DATE DUE

DE 23 '94			
MY 1 '95			
DE 22 '95			
NO 13 '00			
DE 1 8 '00			
DE 21 '02			
NO 10 '05			

DEMCO 38-296

Multicultural Communication Skills in the Classroom

Sol Adler
University of Tennessee–Knoxville

Allyn and Bacon

Boston   London   Toronto   Sydney   Tokyo   Singapore

Cover Administrator: Suzanne Harbison
Manufacturing Buyer: Louise Richardson
Editorial-Production Service: Technical Texts

Copyright © 1993 by Allyn and Bacon
A Division of Simon & Schuster, Inc.
160 Gould St.
Needham Heights, Massachusetts 02194

Library of Congress Cataloging-in-Publication-Data
Adler, Sol, 1925–
    Multicultural communication skills in the classroom / Sol Adler.
        p.   cm.
    Includes bibliographical references and index.
    ISBN 0-205-14654-6
    1. Language and education--United States.   2. Language and
languages--Study and teaching--United States.   3. Intercultural
education--United States.   4. Intercultural communication--United
States.   5. Sociolinguistics--United States.   6. English language-
-Study and teaching--United States.   I. Title.
P40.8.A35   1992
418'.007073--dc20   92-34892
                                                         CIP

Printed in the United States of America
10 9 8 7 6 5 4 3 2   97 96 95 94 93

Contents

Preface

This book is designed to enhance the interface among classroom teachers, speech–language specialists (SLS), and special education professionals who interact with linguistically diverse speakers—the nonnative (as well as limited-English-proficient) and nonstandard-English-speaking children in the classroom. It is the author's contention that speaking in standard English is often intimately related to both academic success and desirable employment.

The reading and writing abilities—the literate skills—of elementary and high school and university students are often related to the oral communication abilities of the speakers. Yet, this interrelationship among the three skill areas is generally neglected.

Similarly, research has documented the negative attitudes and perceptions held by prospective employers regarding the abilities of nonstandard speakers of English who use, for instance, African or Appalachian English dialects. All too frequently they are consigned to low-level jobs regardless of their work potential; in part, this may be related to racial stereotypes for African–American applicants, while "hillbilly" speakers may suffer from geographical stereotypes.

The classroom must be the environment in which standard oral English is effectively taught. To accomplish this task, the teacher must develop appropriate speech–language assessment and management strategies. We believe SLSs can serve as effective consultants to teachers and help them achieve these goals.

This book is designed to be relevant to the professional needs of SLSs and of educators, particularly public school speech–language specialists, and varied educational specialists (e.g., classroom teachers, special educators, remedial reading teachers) in early education classes (e.g., Head Start, kindergarten–third grade). Other teachers in higher grade levels, as well as other professional workers (e.g., psychologists and social workers), will similarly find this book of interest in their professional capacities.

Traditionally, the SLS is trained to treat clients possessing oral communication disorders. During the past few decades, some SLSs have also developed expertise in discriminating between linguistic disorders and linguistic differences and can effectively transmit this information to teachers in their consultancy role.

In the ever-increasing multiculturalism of our country, we find that more and more school-age children possess behaviors related to their culturally diverse memberships. It is therefore incumbent upon us to become sensitive to and aware of these varied cultural influences, particularly the different speaking patterns that permeate our classrooms.

The multicultural issues addressed in this book embrace the theme of multicultural education and are among the most emotional topics confronting teachers and scholars today. Professional workers are grappling with the question of how to convey a greater sense of our country's cultural diversity—including, and in particular, its linguistic diversity—without denigrating or distorting the major role of the Eurocentric culture so predominant in our mainstream way of life.

The determination of some members of culturally different groups to maintain and, indeed, to publicly celebrate the unique mores, values, and behaviors of their culture—including linguistic behaviors—gives support to the nonintervention teaching strategy between client/student and professional workers. We do not support this strategy if it includes linguistic behaviors.

A theme of this book is that the English language, and particularly the standard English* variant of the English language, is a basic bridge to all the different American ethnic, racial, and social class groups—the major determinants of cultural differences in the United States. Furthermore, it is the intent of this book to promote, among other things, an effective way to teach children to speak in standard English through a bidialectal and bicultural teaching strategy, in the belief that this goal can be accomplished by an effective interface between teachers and speech–language specialists.

Accordingly, this book introduces the following themes, which are of particular importance to educators and SLSs:

1. The impact communication differences have upon the acquisition of literacy—acceptable reading and writing skills in English—in particular, when the severity of the communication difference is significant.
2. The need for an effective interface between the teacher and the SLS in their interactions with such children—the nonstandard and nonnative English-speaking children attending our schools. (See Appendix B for a model in-service program.)

Material from some of the articles written by the author, as well as information from a previous text, *Poverty Children and Their Language*, has been incorporated in this book. Previous to its publication, the material in this book was used for many years as class lecture notes in a course, Multicultural Language Issues, the author teaches at the University of Tennessee, Knoxville.

Throughout the text, synonymous usage is made of terms such as culturally diverse, culturally different and poor, and multicultural, and since both terms are in

---

*Standard English is defined as the acrolect of our society; that is, the most prestigious dialect used by educated mainstream American speakers. Nonstandard English usage pertains to the nonacrolects, such as black English or mountain English dialects, which are linguistically *different* but not deficient English patterns. Substandard usage however refers to *deficient* English patterns.

common usage, "African–American English" and "black English" are used interchangeably in the text, as is the case with mountain English, which is also called Appalachian dialect. While speech–language clinician, pathologist, or specialist are variously used, *speech–language specialist* is frequently preferred in this text because it conveys the idea that these professional workers do more than simply treat *disordered* oral communication; they also may teach *different* oral communication skills to nonstandard and nonnative speakers of English.

1

Introduction: Preparing for the Next Century—A Peek into the Future

If professional workers of the next century and beyond are to competently cater to the needs of clients possessing communicative disorders and/or differences, they should be aware of and sensitive to the following: (1) the significant growth of our multicultural population; (2) the growth of nontraditional language-learning environments in which many multicultural children are being reared; (3) the impact of poverty on many of these multicultural children; (4) the speech–language specialist's (SLS) role and responsibility insofar as academic and clinical assessment and classroom and therapeutic management of these children are concerned.

As can be seen in Figure 1-1, there will be meaningful demographic shifts in the age, ethnicity, racial composition, and social class membership of clients and the clinical concerns these shifts may engender. Figure 1-2 shows the emerging multicultural pattern in the United States. Not only will there be a significant increase in ethnic and racial diversity, but it is suggested that in the next century the European–Americans will become a minority group as compared to the total number of other major ethnic groups in our country—the Hispanic–Americans, African–Americans, Asian/Pacific Islander–Americans, and Native Americans. Our need to be sensitized to the mores, values, and behaviors of these varied ethnic/cultural minorities is not a new issue. However, the significant growth of these populations puts new emphasis on the need to change existing clinical practices.

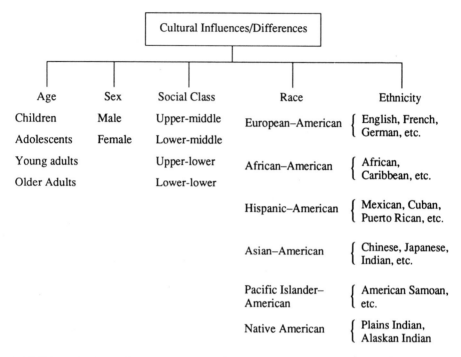

FIGURE 1-1   Some Cultural Influences/Differences in Pluralistic America That May Affect Speech–Language Usage. There is an increase in the Non–Euro–American racial and ethnic groups.

    The nontraditional social environment in which many children are being reared may dramatically alter the nature (i.e., the quantity and quality) of the verbal interactions between caregiver and child. This change, in turn, may have significant impact upon language–cognitive learning and usage. Various substitute caregivers and different language environments are ever more common in our society, and the verbal input by these caregivers in these different environments is an important source of language learning. Said differently, who speaks to the child, what is said, how it is said, and where it is said may affect language development. Studies that have examined the caregiver–child language environment have shown several important characteristics that have correlated with a child's language development (Watson 1989).

    The social-class composition and economic status of people in the United States are changing. This change is characterized by an increase in the class distinctions within the different multicultural populations; there is a growing gap between stable and unstable poor families (Gilbert and Kahl 1987). This cleavage is particularly evident in the plight of the homeless, the economic stresses in the inner cities, "rust-belt" and rural farms, as well as the disorganization experienced by drug-infested

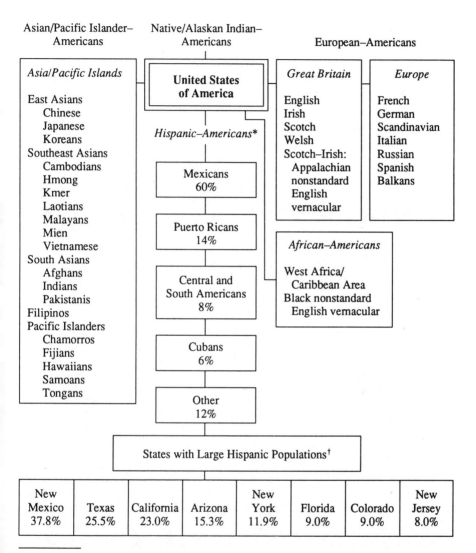

Asian/Pacific Islander–Americans

Native/Alaskan Indian–Americans

European–Americans

Asia/Pacific Islands

East Asians
  Chinese
  Japanese
  Koreans
Southeast Asians
  Cambodians
  Hmong
  Kmer
  Laotians
  Malayans
  Mien
  Vietnamese
South Asians
  Afghans
  Indians
  Pakistanis
Filipinos
Pacific Islanders
  Chamorros
  Fijians
  Hawaiians
  Samoans
  Tongans

United States of America

*Hispanic–Americans**

Mexicans 60%

Puerto Ricans 14%

Central and South Americans 8%

Cubans 6%

Other 12%

Great Britain

English
Irish
Scotch
Welsh
Scotch–Irish:
  Appalachian
  nonstandard
  English
  vernacular

Europe

French
German
Scandinavian
Italian
Russian
Spanish
Balkans

African–Americans

West Africa/
  Caribbean Area
Black nonstandard
  English vernacular

States with Large Hispanic Populations[†]

New Mexico 37.8%	Texas 25.5%	California 23.0%	Arizona 15.3%	New York 11.9%	Florida 9.0%	Colorado 9.0%	New Jersey 8.0%

*The percentage is presented of each discrete ethnic group of Hispanic–Americans. It is estimated that by the year 2000 the number of Hispanic–Americans will have doubled since 1980. Similarly, it is projected that the percent of Asian/Pacific Islander–Americans in our population will have increased from the current 3 percent (1990) to 4 percent in the year 2000 (Ima and Rumbaut 1989). By the year 2000, it is projected that the total African–American population in the United States will be 33 million, of which 2.5 million will be recent immigrants (Robey 1984).

[†]U.S. Census Bureau, 1986 figures.

FIGURE 1-2 Multiculturalism in America: Hyphenated American Speakers

families. Unstable family environments profoundly affect the communicative environment in which poor children are reared.

Lastly, assessment and management practices with the just-noted children will have to be carefully reexamined. Are professional workers interacting properly with such children and their families? To do so will require added sensitivity as well as knowledge of the different cultural mores, values, and behaviors, particularly linguistic and paralinguistic behaviors, of such families. Increased amounts of consultancy interactions will be required if we are to succeed in our work with these children and their families.

Changing Demographic Statistics

Changes in the General Population

As of March 1986, according to the U.S. Census Bureau, the Hispanic population in this country increased approximately 16 percent from the 1980 figure. At the same time, the total national population increase was 3.3 percent. The Asian/Pacific Islander population (who speak hundreds of different languages) increased to 3 percent in 1990 and is projected to increase to 4 percent in the year 2000. It is estimated that by the year 2000, the number of Spanish-speaking people will have doubled since 1980 and that more than 22 million Americans will speak Spanish at the close of the present century. Similarly, the number of African–Americans is projected to increase to 33 million in the year 2000, of which 2.5 million will be recent immigrants from Africa, Central and South America, and the Caribbean Islands (Robey 1984). When one takes into account statistics showing significant growth occurring in other minority populations, the influence and power these minority groups will wield in our school and community activities and planning will be undeniably significant.

As just noted, there will be a great increase in the country's minority populations, particularly school-age children. It follows that there will inevitably be an increase in the number of children speaking a nonstandard or a nonnative English. These demographic changes will require speech–language specialists to address appropriately the assessment and management of communicative deficiencies and differences of multicultural children. Classrooms will be the site in which the management of the linguistic differences takes place; these management issues are discussed in Chapters 7 and 8.

Age Changes in Our Emerging Multicultural Population

There is an emerging age differential in females of childbearing age; that is, there are more young African– and Hispanic–Americans of childbearing age (an average of 25 and 22 years of age respectively) than European–American females of childbearing age (whose average age is 32 years) according to Yates (1988, p. 2). These figures suggest that minority women of younger childbearing age will have the most children in the succeeding generations; thus, the percentages in our population of African–Americans and Hispanic–Americans should show significant increases. "A new baby boom will occur, but this time it will be Hispanic" (Yates 1988, p. 2).

Population Changes in Our Schools

The implications of the aforementioned changes in demographic data in our schools for speech–language specialists and audiologists are quite significant (Cole 1989). At the present time, these professional personnel are mainly European–American, monolingual English speakers. But our country's emerging population characteristics show that approximately one-third of school-age children will be African–American, Asian–American, and particularly, Hispanic–American and that these children will be nonstandard or nonnative speakers of English (Yates 1988, p. 2).

Ramirez (1988, p. 45) points out that there are at least six states with an African–American, Hispanic, Asian, and Native American public school enrollment of 35 percent or more and another twelve states in which these students make up between 25 percent and 34 percent of the enrollment. In some states, minority students now comprise the majority of a particular school grade. For example, in Texas, 51 percent of kindergarten children are Hispanic (Yates 1988, p. 2). Moreover, according to McNett (1983), when all minority peoples are counted, the percentage of culturally different children enrolled in school programs in cities such as Miami, Philadelphia, and Baltimore is 71, 73, and 80 percent, respectively. In summary, by the year 2000, one out of every three students will be African–American, Asian, or Hispanic. Thus, in the coming decades, the multicultural school client may become a major part of the speech–language specialist's case load.

Changes in School Placement and Assessment Strategies

According to Benavides (1988, p. 19), there is a disproportion in the number of racial and language minority students placed in certain special education classes and such placement is often related to the students' socioeconomic, linguistic, and/or cultural heritage. Furthermore, Ortiz and Polyzoi (1988, p. 32) note that ". . . accurately identifying handicapping conditions among limited English-proficient students is difficult." In point of fact, available assessment procedures do not appear to provide adequate information to distinguish second language learners from handicapped students. Thus, the inappropriate placement of multicultural students suggested by Benavides may well be caused by our inadequate assessment strategies.

The traditional speech–language evaluation involves generally an examination of the segmental utterances of the child rather than his/her pragmatic use of language in different situations. Such examinations involving segmental skills may signify handicapping conditions for some clients but for others may reflect a lack of mastery of the English language due to inadequate second language learning. Yet many of these children apparently are being referred by speech–language specialists to learning disability classes and/or other classes for handicapped children (Ortiz and Yates 1983).

Changes in Adult Population

There are currently more than 30,000 individuals who are over 100 years of age and 2.2 million people over 85 years (Yates 1988, p. 1). As our population gets older, it is also becoming less white. Thus, an ever-increasing number of older Americans will be minority language speakers, and there will be a need not only to more effectively address the needs of geriatric clients but, in particular, culturally diverse geriatric clients.

It was pointed out in a series of articles in the April 1989 issue of *Asha* that as the incidence of geriatric clients increases so will the number and diversity of their communicative problems. Clearly, increased sophistication regarding the mores of this demographic entity is required. Similarly required will be appropriate clinical expertise to cater to their nonstandard or nonnative speech, language, and hearing disabilities.

Changing Family Structure: Single Parents, Working Parents, and Surrogate Parents

A particularly significant statistic is the following fact: "For every 100 children born today, 12 are born out of wedlock, 40 are born to parents who divorce before the child is 18, 5 are born to parents who separate, 2 are born to parents who will die before the child reaches 18, and 41 reach age 18 having been raised in a 'normal' family environment" (Yates 1988, p. 2). Additionally, with the continual increase in the incidence of out-of-home working mothers, part-time caregiver responsibilities will shift increasingly to other adults. As this occurs in combination with the data previously noted, it may be that the quantity and quality of the verbal interaction between caregiver and child will change, particularly as more and more children are reared in nontraditional families and in day-care facilities.

For example, according to Watson (1989):

> *Those caregivers ... who produced the ideal motherease ... did appear to view their child as more of a conversational partner in that a high percentage of their utterances were questions which referred to how the child was feeling (e.g., You're hungry, aren't you? or What do you want?). These caregivers who did not appear to be as interested tended to use imperatives which required the child to do as directed (e.g., Look here! or Go get it!). [p.53]*

Thus, the amount of interest in communicating with the child and the types of utterances used are an important factor for providing an optimal environment in which a child can learn language. Watson (1989) also suggests that out-of-home working mothers should consider the type of verbal environment and the types of interactions that take place when enrolling a child in substitute child care. Both Goelman (1986) and McCartney (1984) found that if substitute caregivers do not provide positive verbal interactive environments, there may be adverse effects on the child's language development (see Chapter 3).

In summary, the numbers of multicultural children who attend day-care facilities will probably increase very significantly by the year 2000. The caregivers in these facilities may not be particularly aware of or concerned about linguistic–cognitive learning and, as a consequence, children placed in such programs may not develop their communicative potential. Clinicians should be sensitive to this matter and need to, when indicated, provide day-care personnel with information regarding language learning and usage. This need should be viewed as another facet of the SLS's job description.*

Health State

Socioeconomic status appears to be a fairly consistent correlate of language usage (Adler 1973). Therefore, if the percentage of multicultural lower-class poor citizens increases in our country, there will be a concomitant increase in the incidence of children with communicative needs. Yet, SLSs have limited knowledge of sociological concepts that could enhance their understanding of poverty and the special sensitivity that extremely poor clients need. It is a sine qua non to note the inextricable interrelationship between language and academic learning and the health state of the client. By virtue of their poverty, poor clients need to have attention paid to their health states if they are to function appropriately in our schools.

Disorganized Versus Organized Homes

The generic lower class in America is comprised of a diverse group of peoples: the permanently unemployed, the erratically employed, the underemployed, and the underpaid. In addition, there are the old who are poor, the culturally alienated, aban-

---

*From 1977 to 1979, the staff of the Pediatric Language Institute, Department of Audiology and Speech Pathology at the University of Tennessee, Knoxville, provided information relevant to aural-oral communication to individuals involved in the education of preschool children. The purpose of the program was to familiarize day-care workers in aural-oral language development, disorders, and differences. *A Communication Skills Program for Day Care, Preschool and Early Elementary Teachers* (1982), by S. Adler, D. King, and A. Hodges (Charles C. Thomas, Springfield, Ill.) is an outgrowth of that project.

doned mothers, and the physically, mentally, and psychologically sick, disabled, or different. What these individuals have in common is their economic poverty and, for many, their minority multicultural status. But Pavenstedt (1965), Coleman and Rainwater (1978), and Gilbert and Kahl (1987), among others, have dichotomized the lower-class economically poor into two categories: the upper-lower and lower-lower classes (or the semipoor and the "bottom" lower classes, or the stable and the unstable lower classes). More specifically, children reared in a lower-lower-class home inherit and frequently maintain the sociocultural mores of the family structure, the unstable and disorganized home environment. Such an environment would logically have a detrimental effect upon language and cognitive learning. Contrariwise, children reared in an upper-lower-class home are reared in stable and organized home environments, and this should have beneficial implications for language and cognitive learning. Chapter 3 presents additional information regarding this issue.

Sociolinguistic Heritage

Language emerges as a function of the intermix between biological (psycholinguistic) inheritance and sociocultural (sociolinguistic) experiences. The former is innate and is genetically transmitted in all humankind; thus, at certain ages, particular linguistic stages occur in which children acquire what are termed the deep structures of language. The surface structures are learned differentially by children as a function of their class-cultural membership. Different linguistic rules and strategies are presented to children by adults from different social classes and from different cultures. Thus, children receive linguistic information from their parents, and/or extended family members, and/or housekeepers, and/or day-care personnel—all of whom may be sociolinguistically different. Furthermore, children learn language rules from their peers, either in neighborhood play or in classroom activities. The fact that socioculturally different children bring into the classroom different sets of participatory rules, either linguistic and/or behavioral, should, therefore, not be surprising. All too often, for example, we observe children whose turn-taking or verbal response behaviors are considered inappropriate and perhaps are diagnosed as learning or language-learning disabilities, but which, in fact, are appropriate nonimpaired products of their sociolinguistic heritage (see Chapter 3 for additional information).

Assessment, Management, and Consultancy Concerns

Assessment

Chapters 6 and 8 provide data regarding assessment issues. It is important to recognize that the assessment rules of educators and SLSs will of necessity be altered in the next decade and beyond. As can be seen in Figure 1-3, our clients may be comprised of three different speaking populations—those who speak: (1) standard English, (2) nonstandard English,* or (3) nonnative English (or limited English). As is traditional and current, those clients who come from standard English-speaking environments need assessment instruments that differentiate normal from deficient utterances. But, the nonstandard speaker needs an assessment instrument that differentiates from among those utterances that are either standard, deficient, or culturally different. Lastly, limited-English-proficient speakers require an assessment of their native language functioning as well as their performance in English.

Management

Our interaction with nonstandard speakers will necessitate the treatment/remediation of any *deficient* utterances they may manifest—the SLS's conventional role. In addition, the *different* (but rule-governed) linguistic patterns can be addressed either by ignoring them (the nonintervention approach) or by teaching these speakers to be bidialectal; that is, to develop code-switching behaviors. Chapter 2 explores these issues in much detail. Nonnative or limited-English-proficient speakers will require treatment for any deficiencies noted in either their native and/or acquired languages and the concomitant reduction of foreign accent in the acquired English, as well as the enhancement of the quantity and quality of linguistic patterns spoken in English. Chapter 8 provides much information regarding these matters.

SLSs and Their Caseload in the Public Schools   How many children on the clinician's caseload are nonstandard rather than substandard speakers? How many children possess both nonstandard as well as substandard utterances? Our casual interactions with colleagues throughout the country suggest that all too many of them still adhere to the premise that a linguistic utterance is either right or wrong, correct or incorrect, standard or substandard. Apparently some of our fellow clinicians believe that distinctions between substandard and nonstandard are semantic distinctions of little importance; they also believe that the learning of oral standard English is the primary need of our client population however that need is fulfilled (e.g., the eradication strategy; see page 22 for discussion of this strategy).

Credence is not given to the fact that nonstandard speech–language patterns are legitimate rule-governed expressions of a particular dialectal–cultural community and that these linguistic and paralinguistic utterances should not be eradicated or treated as if they were deficient patterns. This eradication philosophy maintained by some of our colleagues is generally unsuccessful in its stated aim—it does not appear to help the majority of social dialect speakers to acquire and retain standard English. To eliminate, or correct as a deficiency, any aspect of a cultural linguistic pattern is a form of cultural genocide and should be recognized as such (Adler 1979).

The 1983 American-Speech-Language-Hearing Association (ASHA) position paper adequately deals with this concept—that the eradication philosophy is inap-

---

*The regional variants of standard English are *not* considered to be nonstandard utterances.

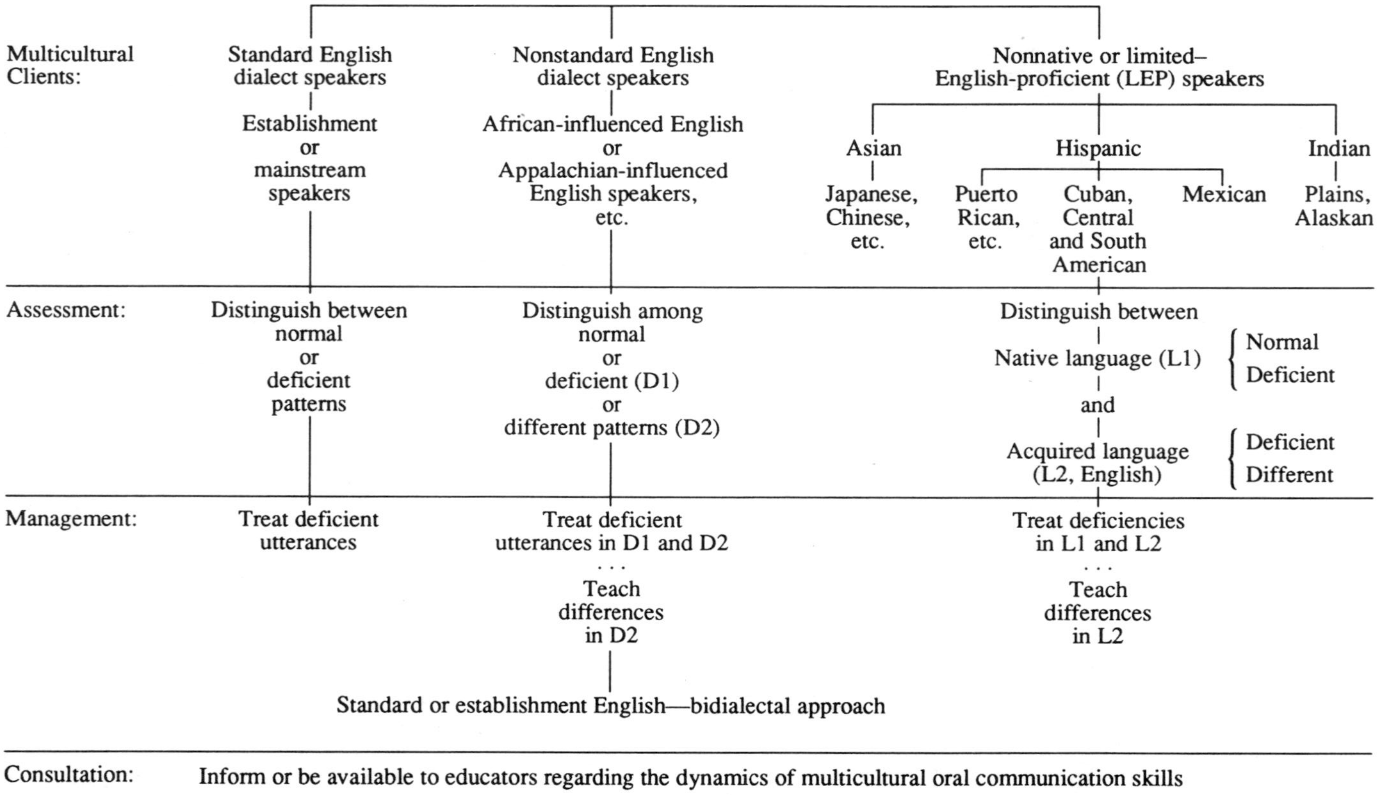

Multicultural Clients:

- Standard English dialect speakers
  - Establishment or mainstream speakers
- Nonstandard English dialect speakers
  - African-influenced English or Appalachian-influenced English speakers, etc.
- Nonnative or limited-English-proficient (LEP) speakers
  - Asian — Japanese, Chinese, etc.
  - Hispanic
    - Puerto Rican, etc.
    - Cuban, Central and South American
    - Mexican
  - Indian — Plains, Alaskan

Assessment:

- Distinguish between normal or deficient patterns
- Distinguish among normal or deficient (D1) or different patterns (D2)
- Distinguish between Native language (L1) and Acquired language (L2, English)
  - Normal / Deficient
  - Deficient / Different

Management:

- Treat deficient utterances
- Treat deficient utterances in D1 and D2 ... Teach differences in D2
- Treat deficiencies in L1 and L2 ... Teach differences in L2

Standard or establishment English—bidialectal approach

Consultation: Inform or be available to educators regarding the dynamics of multicultural oral communication skills

FIGURE 1-3 Implications for the Speech–Language Specialist

propriate. Yet far too many SLSs, we think, are ignoring this position paper. This is both unfortunate and unwise.

Cole's (1983) response to the following question is germane to this discussion:

Question: The administration in my school district and most of the classroom teachers firmly believe in the eradication philosophy. They are pressuring me to regard normal nonstandard English differences as if they were speech and language disorders . . . .

Answer: . . . there are differing opinions [regarding this question]. But the opinion of those who believe in eradication is not consistent with [ASHA]. . . official policy . . . . [p. 27]

What do the public school SLSs and teachers in our country do when confronted by such questions? Specifically, what do they do when confronted by a speaker possessing both substandard and nonstandard verbal utterances? If SLSs decide the utterance is substandard, do they treat the client by presenting only the standard pattern or do they also present the appropriate nonstandard dialectal pattern? If they decide the utterance is nonstandard, do they eradicate, ignore, or teach the bidialectal pattern? Bountress (1980) has shown that the SLS favors bidialectal programming; but how many of the SLSs actively promote its use in the classroom?

In summary, a responsibility of public school SLSs is to ensure standard English usage among dialect speakers. Obviously, ignoring the social dialect or nonstandard utterance does not generate standard or mainstream English; furthermore, the use of an eradicationist teaching style is unsuccessful, perhaps even immoral, and certainly not consistent with ASHA policy. What is left is bidialectalism!

Communicative Disorders in Multicultural Clients

The traditional role of the SLS is to treat clients possessing disordered aural-oral communication. Clients from non–Euro–American populations have, in general, not received the attention their cultural differences deserve from SLSs. The information by Dr. Leith in Appendix F succinctly describes the role of speech clinicians as they relate to stutterers from these other cultures. Clearly, people possessing other speech-language-hearing disorders need to receive similar kinds of attention by professional workers.

Consultancy

Two different articles in *Asha* (Frassinelli, Superior, and Meyers 1983; Garrard 1979) present relevant information concerning the consultative role of speech and hearing professionals in public education. Collaborative interactions with teachers in language arts programs were stressed. Clearly, our intent is to expand upon the services provided by speech–language specialists to classroom teachers by including standard English teaching strategies for linguistically different children. A recent (1991) survey by the author of teachers' knowledge regarding these children revealed a significant lack of information pertinent to dialect usage. The data are presented in Appendix E.

Healey's (1973–1974) "Standard and Guidelines for Comprehensive Language, Speech, and Hearing Programs in the Schools" includes services for children with disorders, deviations, and developmental components. This latter service provides for consultation and demonstration lessons to students regarding their communicative behavior in social, educational, and cultural contexts.

By reinforcing bidialectal usage relevant to school talk (i.e., standard English) and everyday talk (nonstandard English) through consultation with the appropriate school officials including principals, teachers, and support staff, and the demonstration of bidialectal lesson plans, the development of standard English usage in the appropriate cultural contexts can be more readily achieved than is perhaps currently the case.

Is, in fact, bidialectal education of importance? According to Geneva Smitherman (1985, p. 49), it is: "Although the evidence is not definitive, the best available data and expert judgment . . . seems to suggest that . . . only those [African–American speakers] who master code switching make it through the educational system successfully."

Clearly, bidialectal skills are of significance, and their acquisition should not be left to chance. In a consultancy role to the educator, we can provide the information necessary for such acquisition.

The SLS and Bidialectal Training Programs for Teachers   Should public school clinicians be involved in bidialectal training programs for teachers, particularly those in K–2? Obviously, we believe the answer should be "yes," but only if the clinicians involved receive adequate training in their university coursework and practicums. Is this being done? We doubt it; yet this author's seminal article in the *Journal of Speech and Hearing Disorders* (Adler 1971) noted that SLSs must become aware of and receive appropriate training in language differences:

> *Is the providing of such services a proper function for the speech and hearing clinician? If so, it is quite obvious that in order to teach standard English usage, the clinician must first be familiar with the nonstandard . . . components of the speaker's speech and language patterns. [p. 92]*

> *Should we become involved in this problem? . . . It has become increasingly evident that . . . [we] have . . . . The question as posed, then, is a non sequitur; that is, the question is now irrelevant—we are involved! [p. 95]*

We must give voice to our involvement in matters relevant to social dialects. For example, in 1985 the California legislature addressed the issue of dialects in the classroom.* If the bill that arose from this legislative action had been approved, it would have required bidialectal instruction in some classrooms.

According to an article in *Education Week* (1986), "Academic failure by minority students is now so commonplace . . . that many educators have lost the capacity for outrage and the will to cope with this injustice." This statement was generated during a meeting of influential African–American officials, members of the Select Committee on the Education of Black Youth.

This study group suggests that the reason black youth manifest continued educational deficiencies ". . . is that they have been denied the opportunity to acquire the language skills necessary to cross the threshold of learning . . . ." And, according to this committee, there are indications that the problem may be worsening as the gap widens between standard English and the African-influenced English used predominantly by the lower class. Clearly, other culturally different and poor youth (e.g., Appalachians and Hispanics) are confronted by the same problem.

A two-tier system of education has resulted that reinforces the notion that those from culturally and linguistically different lower-class environments are, in fact, of inferior abilities. To negate these influences is of fundamental importance; speech–language "communicologists" can help in this task by promoting bidialectal and bicultural philosophies and concepts, attitudinal changes, and specific teaching strategies to the classroom teacher. In particular, we need to promote our consultancy value to the teacher. Through in-service programs, and other more informal means of communication with the teacher, we should acquaint them with the importance of effective language arts training for nonstandard and nonnative speakers of English. If they are interested in developing such programs, we should provide them with appropriate lesson plans.

Summary Statement

The significant emergence of multicultural clients in the forthcoming years will necessitate an increasing awareness on the part of the SLS that change must occur in some of our traditional assessment and management patterns with these clients. Differences in race, ethnicity, and socioeconomic status require an understanding of a variety of mores, behaviors, and linguistic patterns that may be demonstrated by culturally diverse people. These matters are discussed in Chapter 2.

---

*Specifically, in 1985, the California legislature passed a bill to provide mandatory bidialectal instruction in schools where more than 10 percent of students "lack linguistic proficiency." The bill was vetoed by Governor Deukmejian. (See *Education Week*, September 18, 1985; these data are presented in Appendix C.)

2

Language and Education

The Educator and the Speech–Language Specialist

Dialectal and Attitudinal Differences

Each year children from ghettos, barrios, hollows, and reservations enter our public schools with substantial handicaps in education readiness related to their culturally different heritages. These children bring with them unique experiences and differences in standards and values. They possess a culture of their own with different learning and living styles and different speech and language patterns. The manifestations both of speech and language patterns and of other cultural styles that differ significantly from those used by members of the dominant culture, however, are frequently rejected not only by their peers but also, too frequently, by their instructors. As a by-product of negative attitudes, many students in the public school systems have been labeled functional retardates, and many of these are labeled solely because of linguistic conflicts and cultural differences between them and the teacher. Dialectal and attitudinal differences often result in low academic achievement in the classroom and low scores on intelligence tests. As a result, the role of the educator must also be reexamined. Children born into poverty cultures are being educated by traditional methods in which "correct" expressions of standard English patterns are required. The children are not being given the chance to compare and contrast standard English with their own native dialect or language. Instead, their dialect or language may be rejected as an inferior method of communication.

The author expresses appreciation to Dr. Guy Bailey for his significant contributions to the appendix to this chapter.

Preschool Intervention

A preschool intervention program to introduce linguistically different children to the linguistic patterns of standard English before they reach the first grade would give them a head start. In part, such an early introduction to standard English may enable more multicultural students to succeed academically as compared to the many who presently fail and drop out of school. Most school dropouts are fully capable of achieving in school and their withdrawal from school does not reflect a legitimate lack of ability. Most school dropouts are from lower socioeconomic families and diverse multicultural groups, and many of these children are delayed by at least two years in reading ability—a fundamental educational skill without which no student can perform adequately.

The reasons these children are doing poorly at school in reading and other academic skill areas may be due in part, we suspect, to the language conflicts and attitudinal barriers that exist between them and their teachers. The failure of the child to learn, then, is the fault of the schools—and not of the child. Heretofore, the blame has been placed on the child, who supposedly was deficient in language and therefore in other abilities. Most schools have failed to develop curricula consistent with the environmental experiences of culturally different children, and many times their abilities are seen as disabilities. From the very start the children may be confused and lost. In the first year of school they are being forced to build on a vocabulary they do not possess, they are forced to learn graphic symbols for words they have never before encountered, and they are forced to reason and express themselves in a language that is somewhat foreign to them. If the children were taught basic skills in their own vernacular before they entered the primary grades, some or most of the confusion and feeling of being lost might be eliminated. Or, contrariwise, if the children were taught standard-English-speaking skills in preschool (e.g., Head Start programs) they might more easily make the transition to reading and writing in standard English in their early elementary schooling.

Despite the implementation of numerous early childhood projects for children throughout the country, relatively little attention has been given to the children who enter school speaking a dialect other than that of the broader community in which they live. Many of the current preschool intervention programs are the typical nursery school–kindergarten type, with little alteration other than providing the "deprived" or poor child with environmental enrichment; that is, they try to bombard the children with stimulating experiences that middle-class children receive but poor children supposedly lack. Again, such preschool programs are built on middle-class values and mores and ignore the different needs of economically, communicatively, and culturally different children.

Our Educational Programs and Multiculturalism

Our educational programs generally lack significant emphasis on cross-cultural experiences. Even though Americans are highly exposed to other cultures through the mass media, this exposure is illusory because it is passive. Only by living in a different cultural context, going to school with children from different cultural backgrounds, and experiencing other behavior patterns and cultural traits do individuals become really aware of the cultural distinctions that are uniquely their own and gain respect for those of other people.* If a goal of education is to teach people to learn to function effectively in a multicultural society, multicultural experiences are not only valid but essential. Serious attention should be given to research and demonstration projects that allow teachers and students to gain a new understanding of the nature and importance of cultural pluralism in a democratic society. If we are to be a truly democratic society, we must give each individual an equal place at the starting line. Every minority pupil should be assured that he or she has the freedom to express openly and with pride his or her own unique cultural heritage. This basic freedom is an important prerequisite to addressing the problems of poverty. Therefore, it is evident that programs geared for the poor child are needed, programs that will take into consideration the poor child's own special heritage and, especially, his or her own particular language or dialect so that he or she may compete with his or her middle-class counterpart in mainstream society.

In addition to the kind of program previously suggested, serious attention must be paid to attitudinal problems and learning. For example, Scott (1985), a member of the Black Caucus/National Council of Teachers of English, has noted:

> . . . The language is a barrier in the educational process because of the stigma attached to it, the lack of respect given to it, and the lack of knowledge about it. All of the above factors have been shown to lead to damaged self-concepts of students, low expectations regarding the educability of students, ineffective instructional methods, and sometimes to inappropriate placement of students . . . . [p.64]

These changes can most effectively be accomplished by an interface between the classroom teacher and the speech–language specialist (SLS); that is, a team approach that would allow these workers to coordinate their interactions with the children in the development of bidialectal–bilingual and bicultural programs.

Multiculturalism in the Classroom: Communication Implications for the Teacher

Enthusiasm over alterations in school curricula has diverted the public's attention from the educational problems of children from underclass families. These lower-class children (the culturally different and poor) make up a third of all public school pupils (and educational problems cause many employability difficulties for these youth). The issue is not racial: the high school drop-out rate is high for all underclass

---

*Respect for such differences can best be developed if discussions of these communication and cultural differences ensue in the classroom.

children. This fact suggests that American educators are doing an inferior job educating poor children.

In 1985 Henry Levin, an economics professor at Stanford University's School of Education, warned that unless action is taken quickly to increase the educational and social opportunities for poor children, the economy will be in jeopardy when these same children reach working age without appropriate skills. Hechinger, reporting on this comment in the October 29, 1985 *New York Times*, notes that according to Levin, the current course of raising educational standards for the middle class without significantly improving the education of poor students virtually ensures that the illiteracy problem will grow. It is also forecast that skyrocketing unemployment, poverty, dependence on welfare, epidemic crime, and increasingly violent political conflicts will occur. Other statistics show that 40 percent of 17-year-olds cannot comprehend ordinary documents, 23 million adults are functionally illiterate, and only 29 percent of high school seniors can write a coherent essay. We are rapidly becoming a nation of illiterates.

What Can Be Done

Calls for change in our public education system are evident throughout the United States. As Carl Rowan, the noted journalist, has written, these underclass children are not being taught ". . . the language of society in which they hope to succeed."

What can be done to avert the disaster that will inevitably occur to these children as they grow into maturity? Who is to blame for high school graduates who possess inferior levels of oral, written, and/or reading skills? To place the responsibility wholly on the home, the parents, and the environment is unacceptable; to blame only the teachers is also inappropriate. The unicultural teaching philosophy utilized with these children must be reexamined, and in its place a pluralistic and multicultural-linguistic teaching strategy should be adopted. This teaching strategy entails contrasting the mainstream and the culturally diverse linguistic/communication styles. This comparison allows for the verbal differences between standard and nonstandard English to be auditorially perceived. Such a contrastive analysis strategy teaches the speaker to be bidialectal or to switch dialects according to the linguistic situation.

The Need to Communicate in the Standard Vernacular of Society

If nothing is done to help children become effective standard English speakers (their "school" talk) while retaining their dialects (their "everyday," "home," or "street" talk) they may be severely penalized with respect to their education.

If standard English grammatical rules are learned too late in elementary school, the acquisition of standard English reading and writing skills will be delayed. Informal teacher polls as well as test results, particularly with proficiency tests, indicate that reading skills of dialect speakers begin to show a divergence in the second grade and that the gulf between standard and nonstandard dialect speakers becomes magnified as the child grows older. That there is an intimate interrelationship among talking and reading as well as writing is well recognized; research has clearly documented the existence of a damaging relationship between nonstandard speech and reading and writing problems (Adler 1987, Bergin 1982). Unfortunately, we continue to pay minimal attention to this relationship.

How important is it for prospective job applicants to speak with standard English language and prosody? Some contend that its importance has been exaggerated, that several factors in getting a job take precedence over ability to perform in standard English. But there is little question that speaking in a nonstandard dialect may penalize the applicant for a managerial position or other types of jobs requiring middle-class communication skills. The applicant may be eminently qualified and racial prejudice may not be a factor in the hiring process, yet he or she may not be employed. There are simply too many negative perceptions associated with, for example, African–American English usage. Many attitude studies confirm this—negative expectancies are generated by such social dialect patterns (Terrell and Terrell 1983).

Unless there is an effective bidialectal language arts curriculum in our schools, we shall continue to penalize minority speakers.* It is important to note that Judge Charles Joiner in his landmark Ann Arbor decision in 1979 said, ". . . a major goal of American education is to train young people to communicate both orally and in writing in the standard vernacular of society." We think this is a valid goal. We support it, and we do not believe it can be achieved unless an effective standard-English-teaching strategy is utilized in our schools. It is not racist, but just pragmatically useful.

The Nonstandard-Speaking Child

The publication, *The Story of English* (McCrum, Cran, and MacNeil 1986) depicts this sociolinguistic emphasis. The following quote as published in *The Story of English*, by Constance Clayton, Superintendent of Schools in Philadelphia, expresses this point of view:

> *I consider Black English as a dialect of a particular ethnic group—the Blacks. I consider it incorrect English. I would want an understanding of it, an apprecia-*

---

*Of significance are the number of communities that have essentially adopted these concepts without using this terminology. For example, the Los Angeles, San Diego, and Richmond school systems in California use these ideas but label them oral language arts skills training. But it is important to recognize that language is only one issue and that race alone (even among those speaking standard English) may result in a discriminatory situation. (See Appendix D.)

tion of it, as we would for other dialects . . . but we should never lose sight of the need to provide for our young people access to standard English, which is really a gateway for them to the broader community. [p. 230]

Although there is widespread support of the need for standard English, the conviction that African–American English is incorrect English is untenable in light of current knowledge regarding this subject. (For more information concerning the rules that govern this dialect, see Chapter 4.) Clayton further supports her (and our) position regarding the need for standard English acquisition:

I know of no company or corporation which hires you on the basis of your ability to speak Black English. . . . I have yet to find Black English as being beneficial in filling out a job application. Somehow those questions are not phrased in Black English . . . . That's a very valid reason for the utilization and understanding of standard English. If a person is interviewing you for a job, I think if you said, "I've come to aks you for a job," rather than "ask you for a job," I think the potential employer might be somewhat confused. [pp. 230–231]

According to the authors of *The Story of English*:

The upshot of the Black English debate, which raged throughout the 1970s, was a landmark court decision in Detroit in 1979. In July of that year, the Ann Arbor school district became the first American school system ordered by the courts to take the Black English of the school children into account when planning the curriculum. In his summing-up, the judge gave a remarkably succinct description of our story: "All of the distinguished researchers and professionals testified as to the existence of a language system, which is part of the English language but different in significant respects from the standard English used in the school setting, the commercial world, the world of the arts and science, among the professions, and in government. It is and has been used at some time by 80 percent of the Black people of this country and has as its genesis the transitional or pidgin language of the slaves, which after a generation or two became a creole language. Since then it has constantly been refined and brought closer to the mainstream of society. It still flourishes in areas where there are concentrations of Black people. It contains aspects of southern dialect and is used largely by Black people in their casual conversation and informal talk." To this day, the status of Black English remains a flashpoint in the continuing debate about Black rights. [p. 231]

It is pertinent to note that Judge Joiner (1979), who adjudicated the Ann Arbor case, issued no requirements regarding the teaching of standard English to the plaintiffs in this case. He did mandate, however, that the school board take appropriate action to enhance the children's reading skills. To this end, a series of workshops were made available to the teaching staff in Ann Arbor (see page 26).

Today we find controversy in the orientation of different professional workers; many still believe the environmentally deprived/disadvantaged thesis (and the subsequent need for compensatory or enrichment education) is the sole cause of educational failure (see Chapter 7 for additional information). Other writers, such as Charlotte K. Brooks in her 1985 publication *Tapping Potential: English and Language Arts for the Black Learner*, stress cultural, linguistic, and attitudinal differences and the subsequent conflicts these differences engender in the classroom. We support the latter thesis; we do not denigrate the importance of the environmental limitations thesis, but simply wish to place it in a more proper perspective.

Bidialectalism: Why We Should Implement This Strategy

Linguistic and Cultural Prejudices

It is an unfortunate feature of the American ethos that the dialectal varieties of the ethnic, racial, and lower-class members of our society have been viewed generally with a discriminatory if not a contemptuous perception by the members of the middle-class establishment. In particular, speakers of Appalachian and African–American English have been and still are so stigmatized. So long as linguistic and cultural prejudices dominate the thinking of these establishment members of our society, nonstandard speakers will continue to need to learn the language of the mainstream culture if they wish to have an equal opportunity to enter into the mainstream.

Bidialectal Teaching Concepts

The desirability of utilizing bidialectal and bicultural teaching strategies in our schools for nonstandard speakers is a controversial matter engendering much discussion. If desirable, should the teaching of bidialectal speech–language skills, in particular, be required training in our schools?

This issue is rooted in our nation's history: the proponents of cultural assimilation and the devotees of cultural pluralism are still arguing the merits of their respective positions. In particular, the dialogue between the assimilationists and the pluralists revolves around three issues of importance to speech–language pathologists: (1) social dialect diversity, as a function of racial and social class membership; (2) how this diversity affects the education and employability of nonstandard speakers; and (3) what, if anything, we should do to help such speakers.

Assimilation Versus Pluralism   The term *assimilation* or *acculturation* emerged around 1900 in the context of concern over the nation's capacity to absorb the millions of immigrants who were pouring into the country. Assimilation was used interchangeably with Americanization and was enhanced in 1908 by the Israel Zanger play, *The Melting Pot.* According to Gleason (1984) the term *cultural pluralism* was first coined by Horace M. Kallen in 1915 and expounded upon by Kallen in 1924. His major thrust was to reject assimilative forces since he viewed them as a violation of the democratic ideals and the spirit of American institutions. His writings, moderate in nature, were used by militant pluralists who supported the idea that there is no "national" will, nor should there be one group dominant over another.

At the present time, there seems to be a mixed public reaction to cultural diversity; there also seems to be a resurgence of ethnolinguistic identity—more people are voicing pride in their cultural languages and dialects. But this has not always been the prevailing mood; indeed history teaches us that assimilative forces—nativism—played vital and forceful roles in our country's past.

Militant pluralists reject all aspects of assimilation and affirm the desirability of and necessity of diversity in our system of government. The melting pot protagonists want only assimilation and the removal or elimination of any aspects of cultural differences. Currently the pendulum seems to be swinging on the side of the pluralists, but the forceful rejection of cultural diversity in past years should not be forgotten.

Midway between the extremes of militant pluralism and militant nativism is the melding of these philosophies—their symbiotic relationship. In this symbiosis, each philosophy feeds off the other, allowing for the emergence of a national character and will while accepting many of the various and different cultural mores and behaviors in our country.

Dialect Diversity   The role of dialect diversity in America is undergoing much reexamination. The assimilationists want only one dialect—standard English—as our national dialect. This view is supported by the educational eradicationists who reject any utterance not in standard English. The militant pluralists argue for the coexistence of different dialects; these are the noninterventionists who claim that since the different dialects give cultural identity and pride to the speakers of these dialects, they should not be expected to speak in any other dialect unless they so desire. To compel them to speak in standard English would be a blatant form of racism/nativism according to these protagonists.

Bidialectalism

Higham (1974, p. 68) points out the need for a rapprochement between these opposing forces, a model that "will uphold the validity of a common culture, to which all individuals have access, while sustaining the efforts of minorities to preserve and enhance their own identity." This is akin to the symbiotic relationship just described and supports the bidialectical philosophy of dialect instruction: to teach nonstandard speakers to communicate in the establishment dialect while retaining their own cultural dialect and switching dialect usage according to the communicative situation.

Thus, the perdurable quality of diverse cultural dialects is recognized, but the use of standard English to sustain our national culture is also valued. It is only through bidialectalism that this goal—a national culture—can be achieved. But should the attainment of bidialectal proficiency be mandated in our public schools, or should it be elective (i.e., left to the discretion of the child and/or his or her family)?

Mandatory Versus Elective Bidialectalism

Advocates of mandatory bidialectalism argue that all speakers of a nonstandard dialect of English should be taught standard English while retaining their native dialect. Supporters of elective bidialectalism recommend a choice be given to the nonstandard speaker.

Authors such as Sledd (1969), Hess (1972), and Cole (1985) are opposed to mandatory bidialectalism. Sledd suggests that it is immoral and that it caters to the prejudices of the middle-class whites and supports white supremacy.[1] He supports the nonintervention policy or the do-nothing strategy. This form of reasoning supports the notion that bidialectal training, when obligatory, is racist.

Elective bidialectal services, to the contrary, allow for the learning of standard English to be voluntary and left to the discretion of the child or the child's parents, thereby eliminating any involvement with racist policies. But there are some important flaws in this reasoning. First, many middle-class African–Americans perceive black English as inferior English. (See, for example, an essay by journalist Carl Rowan (1979)[2] and writings of Kenneth Clark, psychologist and educator. Clark, according to Mellan (1970), accuses those who would preserve black English of consigning such speakers to perpetual inferiority.) Thus such writers would probably make the accusation of racism if standard English is not taught to all speakers.[3] Second, all of these arguments pertain to the black English speaker, but obviously would not be appropriate for the Appalachian speaker.

If we allow for elective or voluntary adoption of bidialectalism, it is assumed that: (1) the child or the child's parents can make an intelligent and informed decision devoid of any emotional beclouding of the issue; (2) the teaching of effective bidialectalism in the classroom would not be negatively affected by some parents deciding their children should or should not receive such instruction; and (3) the delay in teaching bidialectal speech–language patterns to some children would not adversely affect their ability to become fluent bidialectal speakers—that is, some parents may want to implement bidialectal teaching for children later than others. The delay in learning standard English grammatical rules would not cause reading/writing problems due to dialectal conflicts. There are those who do not agree with these assumptions!

But the most egregious problem with elective bidialectalism is the suggestion by some that the children can pick up standard English equivalents and become effective standard English speakers without any formalized training. All that is required is the motivation to do so. If this is so there is obviously no need for mandatory bidialectal teaching. Such a supposition suggests and supports a noninterventionist or do-nothing policy in our schools.

Some reject the supposition that follows. They believe that while some nonstandard speakers may attain bidialectal fluency without training, the large majority of lower-lower-class and upper-lower-class school-age children, in fact, do not attain fluency in the segmentals, prosody, and body language of standard English without much help.[4]

The Need for Mandatory Bidialectalism

Educational Reasons

As said previously, informal teacher polls and test results, particularly with proficiency tests, indicate that reading skills of dialect speakers begin to show a divergence in the second grade and that the gulf between standard and nonstandard speakers becomes magnified as the child grows older.[5] Numerous educators, linguists, and speech–language pathologists have stressed the importance of a standard dialect in academic achievement (Baratz and Shuy 1969, Bergin 1982, Johnson 1971, Labov 1969, Wolfram and Fasold 1974). As Hudson (1971, p. 5) states, "The acquisition of verbal skills in standard English is absolutely essential to the child's success in school." Hess (1972, p. 41) comments that "Standard English is an aid to academic achievement."

According to Dabney (1983), the reading ability of low socioeconomic status (SES) African–American students has tended to lag behind the achievement of their higher SES African–American and white counterparts; she also notes that according to the latest National Assessment of Educational Progress, African–Americans (and others) who live in impoverished communities are much less likely to possess acceptable writing skills than are students from affluent communities. These concepts are expanded upon in *Cultural Language Differences: Their Educational and Clinical-Professional Implications* (Adler 1984).

Employment Reasons

Kochman (1969) contends that the importance of speaking in standard English has been exaggerated; he notes that several factors relevant to getting a job take precedence over ability to perform in standard English.

As Cole (1985) points out, the Terrell and Terrell study (1983), which highlights the importance of standard English usage, was not controlled for some other factors, such as dress, and so forth. Therefore, the results of this study must be cautiously evaluated. But in a study by Shuy (1972) in which he studied the responses of employers to taped African–American speakers from middle- and lower-class backgrounds (and therefore using different amounts of African–American English), he found that the employers' ratings also indicated that significant black English usage affects employability. There are simply too many negative perceptions associated with black English or mountain English usage.[6] Many attitude studies (e.g., Harber 1979) confirm this—negative expectancies are generated by such social dialect patterns. Hess (1972), in her review of relevant literature, notes that authors such as Spolsky, McDavid, and Plummer, in different articles, write that it would be naive to assume that a better command of standard English would in itself solve all problems, but that it is certain that the lack of this command is one of the significant causes of frustration and problems in both the school and job environments; that possession of nonstandard dialects has the effect of limiting or confining those who use them.

To suggest that the utilization of a nonstandard dialect is not an important factor in employability is patently misleading. The fact that it is not the only factor insofar as black English speakers are concerned is granted; it is however, clearly an important factor. It is also significant to note that it probably plays an equally important role with speakers of mountain English where there is no potential racist issue involved.

Unless there is mandatory bidialectalism, with all of its social and political negatives, we shall continue to penalize minority speakers in their employability in the "establishment marketplace" as well as their educational development in schools with middle-class curricula.

Ethical and Pragmatic Reasons

Ethical If nonstandard dialects are in fact rule-governed linguistic systems, then the only difference between these dialects and establishment English—the acrolect of English—is that of prestige. Because nonstandard dialects are less prestigious than standard English is no justification to eradicate these dialects. The dialect is a facet of the speaker's cultural identity, and to eradicate any aspect of one's cultural identity and to eradicate any aspect of one's culture requires careful consideration: in a democracy we accept most cultural differences and diversity. But to ignore the pragmatic need to be also able to speak in standard English is to ignore reality.

Pragmatic If standard English is the speech system used by members of the establishment, all members of our society should have the opportunity to learn this dialect system, thereby helping them to enter into the societal mainstream if they so desire. Knowledge of establishment mores, behaviors, dress codes, and speech patterns will ease the difficulties encountered when entering into this society.

Eradicationist teaching does not supply this knowledge effectively. Noninterventionist or elective bidialectalism does not prepare most speakers with appropriate establishment English. Only mandatory bidialectalism can effectively provide both the linguistic and paralinguistic codes of standard English.

Bidialectal Instructional Objectives

The following instructional objectives entailed in the Ann Arbor decision can be used in the formulation of workshop and in-service programs throughout the country (Joiner 1979).*

1. Recognize generally the basic features of a language system as they apply to dialect differences.
2. Be able to describe in general the concept of a dialect and dialect differences within the English language.
3. Be sensitive to the value judgments about dialect differences that people often make and communicate to others.
4. Be able to describe the basic linguistic features of black English as it contrasts with standard English.
5. Show appreciation for the history and background of black English.
6. Recognize readily children and adults speaking the black English dialect.
7. Be able to identify, without prompting, the specific linguistic features by which they recognized a speaker of black English dialect.
8. Be able to discuss knowledgeably the important linguistic issues in code-switching between black English and standard written English.
9. Be able to identify possible instructional strategies that can be used to aid children in code-switching between black English and standard English.
10. Use miscue analysis strategies to distinguish between a dialect shift and a decoding mistake when analyzing an oral reading sample.
11. Be able to describe a variety of language experience activities that can be used to complement the linguistic basic reader program.

Using the Speech–Language Specialist as a Resource Consultant

In our association with a Head Start program and a rural school system (K–3rd grade), we were able to enhance standard English usage and alter the teachers' negative perceptions of the Appalachian English dialect. Our role was to (1) inform the teachers, (2) provide relevant lesson plans, and (3) respond to any prejudices they verbalized.

We obviously believe in the consultative responsibility of speech–language specialists to teachers of nonstandard dialect speakers (Adler 1988). Similarly, Kelli Harris-Wright (1987) underscored the need for such specialists to be actively involved in bidialectal activities in the classroom rather than simply to act as consul-

---

*As noted previously however, an added objective should be bidialectal proficiency.

tants. She notes that a speech–language pathologist was the preferred educational professional to develop the instructional model at the elementary school level, with language arts coordinators serving as resource personnel. (See Appendix I for more information.)

Summary Statement

This chapter underscores the need to teach nonstandard speakers of English to communicate in the standard or establishment dialect of our society. Unless we successfully accomplish this task, some nonstandard-speaking children will be both academically and vocationally impaired because of dialect conflict and negative perceptions regarding such dialects.

In Chapter 6, we present a bidialectal teaching strategy we have successfully used in our contacts with a Head Start program and a K–3rd grade rural Appalachian school system. Not only did the children learn standard-English-speaking skills more effectively than did their peers, but teacher attitudes were significantly altered.

Endnotes

1. For example, Sledd (1969, p. 1309) states in his article that "the basic assumption of bidialectalism is that prejudices of middle-class Whites cannot be changed but must be accepted or indeed enforced on lesser breeds. Upward mobility, it is assumed, is the end of education. But Whitepower will deny upward mobility to speakers of Black English who must therefore be made to talk White English in their contacts with the White world . . . ."

2. In his essay Rowan writes, "The greatest burden Blacks carry in America today, except for the entrenched institutionalization of racism, is that Black children are not being taught the importance of communication—of using the language of society in which they hope to succeed." (p. 5)

3. For example, Marckwardt (1971) states:

> . . . Those who have urged the establishment of a functional bidialectalism as part of the school language program have been charged with hypocrisy and sometimes worse . . . . In general, however, these attacks have been uninformed and naive. Some of them restate positions which any competent student of the language already holds. This is especially true of those who insist that all dialects possess equal value and have an equal right to their existence as media of communication. As far as I know, no linguist has ever called this into question, but no linguist in his right mind could possibly say that all have equal prestige, and there is little point in insisting upon the self-deception that they do. [pp. 33–34]

4. Can children learn effective bidialectalism by exposure to standard English speakers in desegregated schools—schools which have eliminated some racial and socioeconomic

barriers? By the time children reared in linguistic isolation enter the elementary grades, they have learned more than 90% of their unique dialect and its rules. We doubt that exposure to teachers or to standard-English-speaking children, if they are available, is going to be of sufficient motivation or help.

An interesting and relevant article by J. Quinn entitled "Linguistic Segregation" appeared in *The Nation* (November 9, 1985). It presents the results of an interview with W. Labov, the eminent sociolinguist from the University of Pennsylvania. Professor Labov claims that the number of blacks ". . .who are isolated and poor is greater than ever—Blacks who never see a (standard English) speaking White (or Black)" (p. 479), with a few exceptions. In addition, he says, ". . . if we follow our present policies Blacks are going to drift further and further away from the mainstream . . . " (p. 482).

5. This gulf in reading skills is also exemplified in the *Larry P. v. Riles* (1979) California Litigation (C-71-2270) in which black children challenged the continued use of IQ tests as valid criteria for class placement. During the discussion inherent to this litigation, it was noted that ". . . it is not unusual for high school students to be reading at the third grade level" (p. 32). Similarly, Wolfram et al. (1979) have commented ". . . that reading problems seem to be more common among nonstandard English speakers" (p. 1). That educational retardation is disproportionate among the minority poor is exemplified in *Hobson v. Hansen* (1967), as well as the above-noted *Larry P. v. Riles* (1979). In 1982 a report commissioned by the National Academy of Sciences changed the discussion of minority overrepresentation from why does educational retardation occur to why is disproportion a problem. Rather than focus on the issue of bias in testing, the academy concluded that *what kind of educational services were provided to minority poor children* was probably more important than the setting in which such services were delivered (Heller, Holtzman, and Messick 1982; italics added). (See Chapter 8.)

6. For example, in the June 24, 1979, edition of *Sunday Magazine*, a supplement to the *Atlanta Journal and Constitution* newspaper, a reporter by the name of Lee May presents his experiences when applying by telephone for different positions listed in the want-ads. In each case he was rejected for these positions when he spoke in black English to the personnel managers; contrariwise he was asked to interview when applying for the same position speaking in standard English. Was it racism or the pejorative stereotypes that about about nonstandard speakers that caused the rejections? We do not know; we believe however it was probably a combination of racism and negative stereotypical information.

The concern about such pejorative perceptions of nonstandard speakers was exemplified in a workshop sponsored by the Southern Regional Education Board in 1979. Invited to this meeting were faculty and administrators of colleges with significant African–American populations. There were consultants in reading, writing, and talking—the author was the consultant for the latter area. The theme of the conference pertained to the employability problems of African–American graduates from these colleges, as related to their black dialect. Much concern was voiced among the consultants and the audience regarding the problem.

Chapter 2 Appendix

Literacy and the Language Arts: Reading and Writing

> *. . . it is deplorable that so little emphasis is placed on improving oral communication in the English classroom.*
> *Ruth I. Golden,* Ways to Improve Oral Communication of Culturally Different Youth

The Problem

The pivotal problem facing the teachers of culturally diverse children is that they are confronted with dialects that differ from their own and that they usually fail to perceive them as different dialects. To the instructor, all too often, language differences are simply debasements of standard English. These so-called nonstandard dialects vary from standard English in four major areas—phonology, lexicon, grammar, and nonverbal communication.

Phonological differences are the most obvious and stigmatizing, but they are less important as far as a teacher of composition is concerned. Thus, when talking to culturally different children, the teacher will probably notice that ɵ (i.e., unvoiced [th]) is not distinguished from *f* in some cases, and as a result, the students may make homophones of "Ruth" and "Roof." Similarly, some students do not distinguish from *d* as in "the" changing to "de"; others pronounce such words as "it" with aspiration—thus producing "hit." Likewise, the teacher will probably notice that some culturally different speakers tend to simplify and reduce final consonant clusters. Thus "nest" may come out as "ness," "walked" as "wak," and "ask" sounding like "ass." Phonological differences may even extend to the suprasegmental or intonational aspects of language. As a result, the stress is on syllables other than what the teacher expects. Thus, "police," "reform," and "guitar" may be pronounced "po'lis," "ri'form," "gi'tar." Differences in pitch will also probably occur. More importantly, there may be juncture differences—differences in the breaks and pauses in the flow of speech.

Teachers of English are also likely to find that the lexicon of the culturally different child is not familiar to them. For example, how many English teachers would know that to some African–Americans, a "pork chop" is a black who has not lost the traditional subservient ideology of the South? Likewise, instructors might be confused at an African–American's use of "bad" to mean "good" or a white Southerner's use of "carry" to mean "give a lift in a car, or a bike, etc."

More frustrating and not as obvious as phonological and lexical differences are the variations likely to be present in the grammar of the culturally different student. Teachers often throw up their hands in dismay when confronted with "he been drinking," "I burn a hole in my pants yesterday," "the ball is his'n," and "the boy what batted hit the ball." As the preceding examples illustrate, grammatical differences may be morphological or syntactic; they occur in both simple and complex sentences; they are not restricted to any part of speech.

The language differences of the culturally different student even extend beyond language proper; his patterns of nonverbal communications are not those of the middle-class speakers. As we have noted, eye contact, touch, posture, movement, and paralanguage—signals not produced by the articulators or the vocal tract—are ways of expressing emotions and relating social processes.

When dealing with the culturally different, the teacher of English, particularly when teaching composition, is faced with differences in every aspect of language. Not all of these differences are of equal importance, however. Nonverbal communication is, of course, outside the realm of composition, and phonology, no matter how obvious or stigmatizing, is relevant to composition only so far as it affects grammatical matters. Lexical differences would seem to be more serious; on first encounter, they do present barriers to communication, but these are barriers easily eliminated. To find out what a "pork chop" is, we merely have to ask. As far as the composition teacher is concerned, then, grammatical variations pose the most serious problems, for it is on grammatical problems that teachers fail students. If students are to write in standard English, they must master not a particular lexicon or a particular phonology, but particular sentence patterns and morphological systems.

When confronted with the language differences, the teacher of composition has been unable to deal with them—a more serious problem than the differences themselves. The chief reason for this failure is that instructors have failed to recognize that nonstandard varieties of English are just as valid and systematic as standard English; that is, instructors themselves lack the linguistic sophistication to deal with the problem. Lack of linguistic sophistication has led most teachers to a kind of malnutrition theory concerning these language differences: Culturally different speakers lack proper grammatical training and, as a result, their language is some form of debased standard English.

The English teacher, then, faces two problems: the culturally different student has been nurtured in a different dialect, and the teacher does not sufficiently understand either the nature of language or the different dialect. The problems themselves suggest the nature of the solutions.

Solutions

First, it is imperative that teachers understand both the nature of language itself and the nature of dialect differences. Such understanding can best be achieved by developing an interface with a knowledgeable SLS, as noted previously. Also, courses relevant to sociolinguistics would be beneficial. These courses would help shape and mold attitudes and would provide at least some familiarity with various dialects.

Second, teachers must decide just how they are going to approach the problem. Three solutions have been proposed. The first of these maintains that "nonstandard" dialects, regardless of what research in linguistics shows, are inferior modes of communication and, as such, must be eradicated. This solution is based on invalid assumptions about language, and thus it can be dismissed. A second solution, recognizing the fact that no dialect is inherently better than any other, proposes that teachers merely leave the students' languages alone, appreciating the various dialects for what they are. Such a proposal suits the current political climate: pride in the black or mountain dialects is a part of African–American or Appalachian pride in general. Thus, those who tell us to leave these dialects alone accuse eradicationists and bidialectalists alike of racism: the attempts to change one's dialect—especially if one is an African–American—is merely another way of trying to force an individual to become like middle-class whites, to lose his or her identity. As noted previously however, this view overlooks three important considerations. First, standard English is the language of mainstream society; without a command of it one is isolated from the mainstream. Second, standard English is the language of instruction in the schools; it is the language in which all texts are written, and without a knowledge of it, problems in reading and school are likely to occur. Most importantly, however, although there is no standard phonology, or even lexicon, there is a standard written grammar, a kind of koine that serves the whole of the English-speaking world; because of the standard written grammar, Americans can understand a book by Australians and vice versa. Therefore, there seems to be only one possible solution—bidialectalism. This solution assumes that students should learn to write standard English while maintaining the dialect of their nurture.

More linguistic sophistication and the establishment of an approach to the problem is not enough, however. English programs as they now stand must be reevaluated. The program must be based on the needs of the students: textbooks must be revamped to include materials for bidialectal teaching; teaching techniques and methods of evaluation likewise need to be revised.

Teaching Writing

The teacher of English composition is expected to teach students to construct a rhetorically sound essay—one that is unified, coherent, and stylistically appropriate—in any of the modes of discourse or patterns of exposition using standard written English (that koine previously mentioned). These aims are certainly desirable: all students are expected to do written work such as homework, creative stories, research papers, essay examinations, and so forth. The training they receive in composition should prepare them for that work.

A way must be found to avoid dialect interference in composition.* This can

---

*Bergin (1982) found African–American college students enrolled in a freshman composition course received grades highly correlated with the instructor's perception of their oral English. That is, those students perceived to speak with much black English dialect received poor composition grades; those students possessing little black English dialect received good composition grades.

best be done by having students write in their own dialects for the first month or so of the school year. There are a number of advantages to this. First, it allows both student and teacher to concentrate on rhetorical principles and techniques of good composition. In this way, the student can develop good writing skills without the interference a "foreign" dialect causes; good writing skills can be mastered in any dialect. Second, if students are allowed to write in the dialect of their nurture, chances are that they will draw their subjects from their own experience. As every teacher of composition knows, themes drawn from personal experience are likely to be more vigorous and interesting than those about subjects "foreign" to the student. The third advantage is psychological: Students will probably make better grades and thus be encouraged to achieve in school. Furthermore, it is not unlikely that both teacher and student will come to a new appreciation of the so-called nonstandard dialect. The teacher will benefit in another way too. By the time he or she has received five or six papers, he or she will be able to analyze the grammatical, lexical, and morphological differences between the nonstandard dialect and the koine in which the students will eventually be expected to write.

The technique to be used in coming to grips with the various dialects is simply descriptive analysis. For example, if the teacher notes that all or most of her African–American students omit the plural sign *s*, the possessive sign *s*, and the third-person singular *s*, she should conclude that this is a difference in the grammatical systems of these students. At first glance, descriptive analysis would seem a monumental task, but it actually is not. There is only a handful of differences between the nonstandard dialects and the koine. Furthermore, in the case of African–American English, a number of helpful hints have already been compiled.

After three or four weeks the teacher might begin to introduce the establishment or mainstream American English. Do not yet require students to write new themes in this American English; rather, have them "translate" old themes into it. In this way there should be no dialect interference; the learning of a new dialect should not affect the acquisition of composition skills. Then, in classroom work, emphasize the differences between dialects and establishment American English. Using the material collected from student essays, the instructor should be able to illustrate and alert students to divergences in the systems. The use of contrastive analysis and oral–aural drills on specific items—plurals, possessives, their-singular verbs, and negatives, for example—would prove particularly useful.

After about six weeks, students should be required to write compositions in establishment English. By this time, the students should have mastered most of the composition skills they need; that is, they should be able to write unified, coherent, logical, well-supported papers in any mode of discourse. Furthermore, they will have been systematically and progressively introduced to the new dialect; they will have "translated" about six of their papers into the appropriate English dialect and will have been alerted to almost all areas of difference.

We have approached our goals, then, by isolating them and proceeding toward them systematically. The student is taught skills in composition, then introduced to standard English, and then asked to write in it. No matter how good the approach, however, it will probably not succeed if the materials used in the course (i.e., the "reader") are not geared to the culturally different student.

Teaching Reading

Almost every English class, at the secondary level in particular, makes use of a book of reading selections. These selections are supposed to serve two purposes: (1) to provide illustrations of various modes of discourse and expository patterns, and (2) to provide models for the proper use of the language and rhetorical and stylistic techniques. Now if all papers are written in standard English and students are allowed to write in the dialect of their nurture, it is obvious that the reader cannot fulfill the latter of these functions. The problem, then, is to find a reader that, while furnishing illustrations of various modes of discourse and patterns of exposition, provides relevant models for students' language. That is, we need a reader that caters to culturally diverse children.

Many times readers are organized around particular themes. For example, one well-known reader at the upper secondary and college level is organized around work and leisure, another around cultural decay, and a third around the essay as an instrument of modern culture. The reader for our course might be organized around the theme of cultural diversity; that is, it should examine the various cultures that coexist in America. It might treat comparatively the various institutions that make up cultures. For instance, stories about the ghetto, hollow, barrio, and suburb might be included. There might also be essays on family life, literature, entertainment, and so forth. Most importantly, though, there would be selections on the various languages or dialects of these cultures. Furthermore, these essays should prove useful in approaching the study of language.

The readers, then, should reflect the variety of mores and values that permeate American society. Thus, in reading these selections, students should learn about something other than modes of discourse—although they should surely learn that too. The reader itself will establish a pluralistic base for our approach to composition.

Most importantly, though, a large number of selections must be written in dialects that are spoken by the multicultural children in the classroom. If this is the case, the students will have viable models to work with, and the instructor can really illustrate the cultural diversity of our society.

Our readers, then, are organized around the theme of cultural diversity, reflect the various mores and values of different cultures, illustrate various modes of discourse, *and are composed in a variety of dialects.* The possibilities for discussion and the theme topics that arise from them should be infinite. For example, questions following the selections might be divided into three categories: questions on the mode of discourse, questions on the language, and questions on the institution and culture the selections discuss. The teacher should always ask students how the languages of the readings differ both from their own—if indeed they do differ—and from standard English. In this way the students will be made aware of differences in systems. Furthermore, students can be asked to translate passages of the essays into other dialects. Questions on subject matter should provide topics for student essays. For example, the student may wish to compare and contrast an institution of his or her culture with one treated in the reader.

A reader geared to the problems, needs, and interests of the culturally different will go a long way in solving the teacher's problems. When used with the approach and techniques suggested, in our opinion, the results will be phenomenal. Moreover, our approach should eliminate many of the problems the composition teacher has in grading and evaluating the culturally different student. Dialect interference would be eliminated, grading norms would be altered so as to be based on the peer group, and we would not have to foster the myth of "correctness." Most importantly, though, the course is built upon the idea of progression. Goals are isolated and approached one at a time. When one has been met, students then begin work toward the next. What we have, then, is a program that is pedagogically sound, psychologically beneficial, and structured to meet the needs of students.

Although teachers of English are presently faced with the most critical problem they have ever encountered, it is not a problem that cannot be solved. It is true that for the most part, they are teaching students whose values and languages differ from their own. However, if the teachers will take it upon themselves to obtain the necessary linguistic sophistication and sympathetic understanding, they will have provided themselves a solid foundation from which to work. If they will restructure their courses—redefine aims, refine approach and technique, and revise materials—they can effectively educate culturally different children and can teach them the composition skills necessary in future vocation or college work. The problems of these children are not only theirs; they are ours.

3

Language and Sociocultural–Linguistic Concepts

Intercultural Communications

The systematic study of what happens when intercultural interactions take place during assessment and/or management sessions is the focus of this chapter. The significant growth of culturally diverse populations in this country makes such a study very important. The forces of change in the United States will cause increased contact among different cultural groups and require that speech–language specialists (SLS) develop communication skills, abilities, and sensitivities appropriate to a true multicultural society.

Terminology and Labeling Issues

Terminological Issues

Frequently, the terms *culture*, *ethnic*, *racial*, or *social class* are carelessly used. Following are more rigorous and yet functional explanations.

Culture can be defined as any group of people who share a common history and a set of relatively common behaviors and/or communication patterns. Similar ethnic, racial, and/or social class memberships create cultural groupings. Culturally diverse SLS/client relationships occur when there is a difference in the ethnicity, race, or social class (as well as sex and age) membership of these individuals. *Ethnicity* is based upon one's ancestry, religion, or nationality. According to Lampe (1988), an ethnic group may be defined as individuals who share a common history or tradition, a sense of peoplehood, or a common way of life. *Race* refers to the physical classification of humankind; a racial group is characterized by some combination of physical characteristics. Members of the same race often share the same culture, *but no common culture is found among all the members of any racial group*. Race is based on nature while culture is based on nurture. *Social class* membership is generally dependent upon socioeconomic factors, such as one's income, education, and/or employment. However, other indexes can be used to ascertain class membership such as sociopsychological factors and/or sociolinguistic patterns: how people behave and/or how they talk.

As said previously, these interracial, interethnic, and/or interclass interactions between SLSs and clients may generate feelings of superiority on the part of the SLSs; that is, the cultural beliefs, social patterns, and behaviors, including linguistic patterns of the SLS, are considered correct (or desirable or proper) while those of the client or student are perceived as incorrect (or undesirable or improper). Such biased stereotypical relationships may well affect the reliability of the assessment and perhaps cause ineffective or inappropriate therapy progress. Figure 3-1 presents these relationships. The former problem is suggested in the research of Fuchs and Fuchs (1989), who found African–American and Hispanic–American children's test scores were significantly higher when the testers were familiar interactants, that is, from the same race and ethnicity.

Labeling Issues

Feelings of Superiority   The atmosphere permeating an assessment/management interaction between different interethnic, interracial, or interclass interactants may well be negative when a "we–they" perception is created. This kind of negativeness may be created when labels such as "black" or "Chicano" are used rather than African–American or Hispanic–American. According to Lampe (1988), these behaviors—the essence of general semantics*—are significant and should be recognized as such by clinicians.

---

*Alfred Korzybski (1948), the "father" of general semantics, used the term "time binder" to distinguish humankind's use of and transmission of labels and their effects. That is, peoples from different cultures pass on to their heirs these different labels and these unique effects. Said differently, the most precious of all cultural legacies we transmit to our heirs is the system we use for codifying sensations and experiences. Both consciously and unconsciously we teach each succeeding generation their perceptual orientations, cognitive biases, and communicative codes. The ethnocentric beliefs we also transmit suggest to these generational offspring the propriety of these orientations, biases, and codes. These dynamics greatly influence our interactions with culturally different clients.

Example of Typical Clients

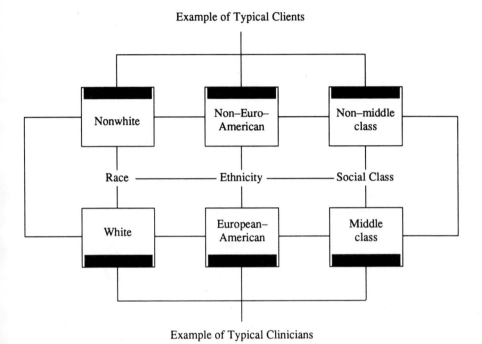

Example of Typical Clinicians

= Clinicians or clients who are of different race and/or ethnicity and/or social class possess a sufficiency of *common* characteristics that allow them to be members of a common culture—the American culture.

= Clinicians or clients who are of different race and/or ethnicity and/or social class possess a sufficiency of *different* characteristics that allow for the formation of distinguishable subcultures. Interactions between clients and clinicians of different subcultures may produce communicative distortions.

FIGURE 3-1   Cultural and Subcultural Identities

Feelings of Prejudice   Lampe (1988) also notes that interethnic interactions between peoples (e.g., SLS/teacher and client/student) may be seriously affected by prejudice, more so it would seem than are interracial or interclass relationships. This prejudice may be particularly manifested in nonverbal behaviors that are both subtle and covert. It is difficult to mask these feelings, and SLSs and teachers should be very conscious of this potential problem during all interactions.

Feelings Caused by Stereotyping   People generally react to their perceptions of reality and not to reality itself; thus the experiences we have had "color" our view of people and events. A plethora of research indicates that people from different cultural groups often possess unique perceptual experiences and that these perceptions create stereotypes that engender specific feelings. These stereotypes and feelings may obviously affect the relationship between the SLS/client or teacher/student.

The Twenty-First Century

There will be a significant alteration in the composition of our country's population and this change will be manifested as well in the professional worker/child interaction. That is, as is currently the case, the large majority of SLSs will likely be Caucasians of European–American extraction and be from the middle socioeconomic class whereas clients will be members of culturally dissimilar groups.

Demographers estimate that by the middle to third quarter of the twenty-first century, a majority of American citizens will trace their roots to Africa, Asia, the Pacific Islands, or, and in particular, the Hispanic world—Mexico, Puerto Rico, Cuba, South and Central America, or the Caribbean Islands. This drastic demographic increase, as well as the relative status quo of the white European–American population, is of critical significance to our political as well as our educational and habilitational systems. As we experience increasing numbers of different ethnic, racial, and class cultural contacts in our various assessment and therapy-educational programs, will tensions caused by cultural misunderstandings be exacerbated between child and clinician? Unless we make a determined effort to educate professional specialists to the potential difficulties involved in intercultural communications, we may well encounter such a future.

The Hispanic–American Client/Student

Of particular importance are our contacts with Hispanic–American clients. The historic movement of millions of Hispanic immigrants during the past and future decades and the variety of racial and ethnic groups that constitute its population today, make the United States a unique study in race and ethnicity. While Caucasian Hispanics currently constitute a small percentage of Spanish-speaking Americans, it is predicted that the "Browning of America" will occur in another three to four generations; that is, the nonwhite Hispanic ethnic group will become a major demographic entity, if not the majority race in America.

Generically, the term *Hispanic* refers to persons born in the United States of families of Spanish-speaking heritages—whether or not they speak Spanish. It may also be used to label people whose names denote a Hispanic heritage. Literally however, the term refers to persons from Spain or Spanish-speaking countries. Peoples of different races, ethnicity, and social class comprise the Hispanic population in the United States. At present about 7–8 percent of the U.S. population is estimated to be Hispanic–American. In another few generations, it is *conservatively* predicted that Hispanics will comprise about one-quarter of our population. "By the year 2020, the Hispanic population is expected to surpass the Black cohort to become the largest minority group in the nation" (Fradd and Correa 1989).

There has been a fair amount of research on the varieties of English and Spanish spoken by Hispanic–Americans in the United States (Duran, Emight, and Rock 1985). For example, two nonstandard forms of English are spoken by Southwest Hispanic–Americans: Pachuco or Calo and Chicano English. In addition to these latter forms of English some Hispanic–Americans speak African–American English, as well as a fourth variety of English, namely standard American English. Outside the Southwest, there are spoken varieties of Spanish, such as Puerto Rican Spanish, Cuban Spanish, Isleno, and Ladino (Judeo–Spanish). Specific regional Hispanic dialects also exist, such as Nuyorican English, spoken by some Puerto Ricans in New York. (Differences between Spanish and English are presented in Appendixes G and H.)

Thus, in the twenty-first century, there may well be an exacerbation of differing cultural interactions between professional specialists and peoples from differing cultures and subcultures, particularly with differing Hispanic–Americans. These contacts may well cause conflicts due to ethnocentric beliefs.

Cultural Conflicts and Ethnocentrism

As noted previously, the terms *culture* or *subculture* refer to societal norms and practices that allow for certain behaviors and beliefs or ways of living. Said differently, when a way of life is shared by an entire society, it is a culture; contrariwise, a subculture is limited to a distinguishable segment of that society (e.g., men or women, young or old, etc.) that has much in common with the dominant culture, but also possesses some unique features (Gelfand and Fandetti 1986). A person's ethnic, racial, or social class membership (as well as gender and age groups, etc.) may determine one's unique cultural and subcultural identity. Different subcultural systems allow for the acquisition of patterns of conduct that permit successful adaptation to their existential world; that is, conduct that allows members of a given culture to deal effectively with their environment. Those SLSs and children from different subcultures may possess differing methods of dealing with their common problems or differences; because of ethnocentristic beliefs, this may lead to communicative breakdowns.

A unique feature of one's cultural or subcultural membership is ethnocentrism—the belief that one's societal conduct and norms are superior to those held by members of other cultural groups. Given the fact that most SLSs are members of European–American ethnic groups, are Caucasian, and are from the middle socioeconomic class, it should not be unexpected that some cultural conflicts between SLSs and culturally different clients may be overtly or covertly manifested (see Figure 3-1).

The SLS and Intercultural Communications

As previously suggested, the ethnocentric feelings of the SLS toward a culturally different client may negatively affect an assessment interaction or a therapy relationship.

It is important that the SLS be sensitive to this possible reaction, which is often institutionalized and covert and triggers both the Rosenthal and Hawthorne effects: respectively, "expect less effort or result from culturally different clients and therefore obtain poorer performance," and "expect poorer performance and therefore pay them lesser amounts of attention." Because a client's adaptive mechanisms, appearance, speech-language patterns or style, or income/educational levels may be different from those of the clinician is obviously no reason to suspect or believe that the client is from an inferior social–cultural group and is not deserving of the same expectations and same attentional level as are culturally similar clients. "Behaviors, then, should be analyzed in these terms: how successful are they in providing the means to cope with problems? Such analysis must proceed without the imposition of artifactual conclusions—without our own institutionalized concepts of right or wrong imposing themselves onto our evaluation of those different behaviors" (Adler 1979, pp. 3–4).

There is a reciprocal relationship between culture and communication: One cannot exist without the other; one cannot change without causing change in the other. That is, differences in social perceptions by either client or clinician may affect the meaning inherent in a message transmission by the intercultural communicants. Unintended errors in meaning can occur because people with different sociocultural backgrounds may interpret the message differently than intended by the encoder. For example, anthropologist Edward T. Hall (1976) categorizes cultures as being high context or low context. In high context cultures, such as Japanese or Arabian, people tend to be very much aware of their surroundings and hence do not rely on verbal tools as their main or only source of information during communication. To the contrary, Americans are generally low context peoples who very much rely on verbal sources of information. Obviously, communicative difficulties can ensue between high and low context communicants.

Nonverbal Communication

In addition to the different verbal patterns used by multicultural Americans, there are also nonverbal components that may differ significantly, and these nonverbal messages can influence the clinician-client communicative transaction. Differences in kinesics (body position, body orientation, facial expressions, and gestures), oculesics (eye movement and position), haptics (touch), proxemics (spatial relationships), and chronemics (time or temporality) may enhance or detract from the intended message and precipitate conflicts. For example, some of the differences involved in proximics and smiling behaviors have been investigated. Dolphin (1991) points out that different researchers have found significant differences in body space patterns or proximics when same-race dyads are compared to different race dyads. For example:

As early as 1990 . . . differences for personal space needs [were noted] in Hispanic–American, White-American, and Black-American children, with mixed race dyads exhibiting greater distances than any single race pairs. In studies of black and white children, (it) was determined that by age seven, black children require less personal space than white children . . . .

[Researchers] observed 210 same-sex first and second grade dyads from three diverse New York City subcultures: blacks, whites, and Puerto-Ricans . . . . [They found that] whites maintained distances nearly twice that of blacks and Puerto-Ricans. [p. 327; emphasis added]

Barna (1991) points out that international students vary with regard to smiling behavior:

Japanese student: *On my way to and from school I have received a smile by nonacquaintance American girls several times. I have finally learned they have no interest for me; it means only a kind of greeting to a foreigner. If someone smiles at a stranger in Japan, especially a girl, she can assume he is either a sexual maniac or an impolite person.*

Arabian student: *When I walked around the campus my first day many people smiled at me. I was very embarrassed and rushed to the men's room to see if I had made a mistake with my clothes. But I could find nothing for them to smile at. Now I am used to all the smiles.*

U.S. student: *I was waiting for my husband on a downtown corner when a man with a baby and two young children approached. Judging by small quirks of fashion he had not been in the U.S. long. I have a baby about the same age and in appreciation of his family and obvious involvement as a father I smiled at him. Immediately I realized I did the wrong thing as he stopped, looked me over from head to toe and said, "Are you waiting for me? You meet me later?" Apparently I had acted as a prostitute would in his country. [pp. 346–347]*

As evidenced in these examples, the lack of comprehension of nonverbal signs and symbols is a definite communication barrier.

The SLS and Client of Tomorrow: A Summary Statement

It would seem to be most critical that we find ways of gaining entrance to the existential and communicative worlds of peoples from other cultures to understand the norms that govern face-to-face relations and to prepare clinicians to function within cultural systems that are foreign but no longer incomprehensible. Without this knowledge and the insights gained from this information, we condemn ourselves to remain cultural outsiders and thereby promote a subtle cultural arrogance as we deal with multicultural clients.

Cultural arrogance—the ethnocentrism previously alluded to—is a dangerous form of provincial naïveté. We must not allow ourselves or our profession to fall heir to such a legacy. As we experience increasingly frequent culturally different contacts, we need greater factual knowledge of each culture, including the need to grasp the way that other cultures perceive the world, and the mores and values that are the foundations to these perceptions. This information will allow us to more effectively relate to our current clients, and particularly future clients. To obtain this information, we should encourage our students to take diverse cultural anthropological and sociological courses during their undergraduate education programs.

In summary, there are six important causes of communicative breakdown across cultural boundaries that the SLS must be aware of:

1. The assumption of similarities between speaker and listener rather than differences; the reverse is also a possibility—that is, the assumption that differences exist between speaker and listener
2. The use of different verbal language patterns and subsequent misunderstanding
3. The use of different nonverbal language behaviors and subsequent misunderstanding
4. The presence of preconceptions and stereotypes and resultant prejudice
5. The presence of preassessment beliefs and the resultant Rosenthal effect
6. The presence of premanagement beliefs and the resultant Hawthorne effect

Social Class and the Sociocultural Bases of Language

The term *social class* refers to those distinctions and differences that stratify people into different groups; for example, socioeconomic status (SES), sociopsychological behavioral patterns, and sociolinguistic verbal factors are social class determinants. Of particular interest here is the apparent increasing amount of conflict regarding these social-class categories with respect to language development and language pathology. Thus, there is a need to reexamine some of the basic assumptions undergirding the relationships between social class and language.*

Such reexamination is especially relevant at this time since class stratification

---

*The social-class bases of language acquisition and usage in children pertains to the relationship between adult caretakers of different social classes and their use of differing types and amounts of linguistic and cognitive stimulation during their interactions with children. The fact that some parent, day-care worker, or other parent surrogates may be of middle social class membership and others from the lower social class does not necessarily mean that some children will acquire and use language in a superior or inferior manner. What matters is the frequency, nature, and motivation involved in the linguistic interaction between caretaker and child. Simply put, because an adult possesses high income, job status, or educational level does not necessarily relate, in a positive way, to language. These socioeconomic factors are only significant if they provide for an environment in which much parallel talk, self-talk, modeling, and other types of nondirective linguistic stimulation are manifested and if the adult motivates the child to want to learn language patterns.

Ethnicity/Race	Social Class Membership			

Ethnicity/Race	Middle		Lower	
1. European–American 2. African–American 3. Hispanic–American 4. Asian/Pacific Islander–American 5. Indian–American	Upper- middle	Lower- middle	Upper- lower	Lower- lower
	None	Some	More	Much

Amount of Dialect

FIGURE 3-2   Cultural Membership. In general, the amount of nonstandard dialect in multicultural American speakers as a function of social class membership.

and subsequent class rankings appear to affect our behavioral management and habilitative relationships with children, that is, the Hawthorne and Rosenthal effects. The Hawthorne effect involves people responding favorably to the greater attention they receive in being the object of the investigator's or teacher's interest; the Rosenthal (Pygmalion) effect involves people changing in the direction they think the investigator or teacher wants them to. In our society in general, culturally different and poor children tend to receive lesser amounts of attention and/or meet with a lower level of expectation. Thus, poor or lower-class children whose social, racial, or ethnic status differs from that of the investigator or teacher may suffer accordingly because of overt or institutionalized prejudices. Many of these prejudices are related to invalid and untenable assumptions regarding these children. One of the most apparent and damaging is that the speech and language of the lower class is an inferior verbal pattern characterized by many articulatory deficits, grammatical errors, and lexical inadequacies. To the contrary, many of these so-called deficits are in fact nonstandard utterances that have been incorrectly diagnosed. Figure 3-2 shows that, in general, the amount or quantity of nonstandard dialect patterns is related to the speaker's social-class membership. As a consequence of this assumption, compensatory speech, language, and educational programs have been instituted in many schools. According to some writers, compensatory programming has failed; its failure may well be related to its invalid foundation. We accept the fact, however, that many cliches regarding culturally different children and their families, although lacking validity, automatically trigger drastic educational and habilitative strategies.

Socioeconomic Factors

Validity of the Factors

The most common factors used in judging economic social class differences are (1) occupation, (2) education, and (3) income. Other and less frequently used criteria are rent and the value of one's home. That these criteria allow for valid social class distinctions are questionable; nevertheless, most researchers use them.

Earnings   That the criterion of earnings may be a particularly prejudicial factor is of concern for members of cultural minorities since a significant discrepancy has been noted to exist between occupational level (i.e., earnings) and educational achievement. For example, it is not uncommon for African–Americans, Hispanic–Americans, or females who possess relatively high levels of education to be unable to obtain employment commensurate with their education. Earnings, furthermore, are based solely on income generated by the father in many stratification systems. This kind of chauvinism does not allow for an adequate social class portrayal of matrifocal homes in which the mother is the breadwinner or, for a more common current practice, situations in which both parents contribute to the economic well-being of the family.

Education   Educational attainment is measured in our census statistics according to years of schooling completed. No distinction is made, however, for differences in the quality of training provided or received as well as for the quantity of education attained. Thus "years of school completed" may mean vastly different things; education, after all, is not synonymous with time spent in the classroom. It is well recognized that the quality of education provided for or received by nonwhite ethnic and lower-class groups has been generally inferior. Nevertheless, the quality of education as an important criterion is not considered in social class ranking.

Homogenization of the poor   As noted in Chapter 1, the homogenization of the lower-class respectable and downgraded poor is particularly a problem for those who desire to measure and quantify discrete behaviors both unique and common to members of the different subcultures of the "culture of poverty." The better known SES stratification systems do not allow for valid characterization of the lower-lower class—the unstable or underclass poor. Those who are interested in obtaining information regarding language development and language use in children from these discrete subcultures have had difficulty in finding a valid system that allows for proper and rigorous identification of them. We have found it useful, however, to distinguish between the upper-lower and lower-lower social classes by the stability or instability of the home environment; the presence of a father figure frequently, but not necessarily, generates well-defined and coordinated behaviors among the various family members. Additionally, the quantity of maternal education may be an important factor in discriminating between the social classes and the nature of the home environment. These criteria are not sufficiently objective to allow for rigorous identification. We need quantifiable measures that would remove or attenuate much of the subjectiveness now inherent in the stratification system.

Validity of Molar Stratification Systems

The significant differences in value systems and mores within the middle and the lower classes as a result of ethnic, racial, economic, and geographic factors may not be as gross as those between classes; nevertheless, the fact that there are differences has been well documented. Utilization of the conventional molar stratification system—that is, middle vs. lower class—smothers these differences and may contribute to an uncontrolled bias in research studies. It follows that if a researcher has only middle-class children, per se, for his study, he may inadvertently be utilizing children from mainly the upper-middle or from the lower-middle class. To suggest, then, that the results of the study can be generalized to the middle class en toto is perhaps an unwarranted assumption. This criticism is perhaps even more relevant to the lower class, in which a more significant dichotomy may exist.

We do not suggest that such generalization are always valid: we only suggest caution. Some of our pilot studies have suggested, for example, that upper-middle-class children may be superior to lower-middle-class children on the Peabody Picture Vocabulary Test-R. We have noted also the possibility that, on some tasks at least, the lower-middle-class and upper-lower-class child may be more similar to each other than to their respective class peers. As a matter of fact, there may well be three significant stratifications in terms of socioeconomic criteria: (1) the upper-middle class, (2) the lower-middle and upper-lower classes, and (3) the lower-lower class.

A Recommended Stratification System

There is simply no one measure or combination of measures that is a strong predictor of language behavior. In our own research we use the maternal education level and divide the social classes as follows:

Level 1	Upper-middle class—13 years of school and over (college)
Level 2	Lower-middle class—high school
Level 3	Lower class—0 to 9 years (elementary and junior high)
Level 4	Upper-lower class—6 to 9 years (elementary or junior high)
Level 5	Lower-lower class—0 to 5 years (only some or no elementary)

Even though education often serves as the single factor for SES position, the information regarding occupation may also be utilized; it is tabulated according to the following criteria:

Level 1	Upper-middle class (professional, managerial)
Level 2	Lower-middle class (trade)
Level 3	Upper-lower class (laborer)
Level 4	Lower-lower class (chronic welfare aid, street people, disorganized homes)

In addition to these formal criteria regarding socioeconomic status, a sociopsychological analysis of lower-class position is made by virtue of the home environment or life style. Thus, for level 4, upper-lower (in the education system) allows for a stable, organized environment that provides linguistic and cognitive stimulation. For level 5, lower-lower, there is an unstable and fairly disorganized environment; there is little in the way of any kind of organized stimulation.

Sociopsychological Factors

Verbal Factors: The Type, Quality, and Quantity of Verbal Stimulation in Culturally Different Homes

Many authors suggest that the amount, type, and quality of verbal stimulation and cognitive enrichment encountered in lower-class homes is inferior to that manifested in middle-class homes. This statement is a gross oversimplification, but many people have accepted its validity. Many maintain also that because of the value system of middle-class culture, parents play a major role in teaching their young so that, by the time they reach school age, these children have achieved a relatively high level of language ability. That is, their parents talk to them, read to them, and, in general, foster a verbal give-and-take that helps the children develop their potentialities. Numerous articles can be cited to support the contention that the verbal environment of the middle-class child is superior to that of the lower-class child's environment.

In the literature we find very little direct observation of verbal interaction in any subcultural member's home; most typically, the investigators ask the child if he has dinner with his parents and if he engages in dinner-table conversations with them. He is also asked whether his family takes him on trips to museums and other cultural activities. This slender thread of evidence is used to explain why the environment is considered linguistically impoverished.

In fact we do not know the relative benefits or disadvantages of the type, quality, and quantity of verbal stimulation in culturally different homes. To suggest that all lower-class members (i.e., upper-lower or lower-lower class) manifest the same pattern of verbal stimulation seems to be a patent absurdity. Although there are bound to be many similarities in linguistic behaviors, there are also significant differences. Furthermore, much of the information available has been obtained through retrospective-type questionnaires, and the reliability of such a data-gathering technique is notoriously suspect.

More specifically, it is said that the lower-class child, in comparison to his middle-class peer, has less verbal play and receives less verbal interaction and reinforcing behavior. Therefore, the lower-class child's speech and language development is retarded or deficient. *Such assumptions are generally based on data obtained from retrospective questionnaires, not from field observations relevant to the nature of the verbal interactions in specific homes.* For example, the seminal study by Young in 1970 found that poor black families in a small community in Georgia tend to hold their babies during the first year of life more frequently than do mothers in middle-class families; furthermore, the position in which the baby is held allows the baby and mother to see each other and thus encourages many verbal interactions. Such enhancement of the "prelinguistic" or "babbling" period may have significant impact upon the baby's future language development.

Young also found that the time period from one to two years—also known as the "knee-baby" period—is a time when the baby receives much less attention from the mother relative to the previous year, a period during which the baby is allowed to crawl around with much more freedom than in the typical middle-class home. Similarly, during the time period from two years to the schooling years, the youngsters are monitored by an older child, a child know as the "nurse-child."

These latter periods, the knee-baby and the nurse-child periods, might be said to be inferior in terms of the type and amount of verbal stimulation the child receives in comparison to the quality and quantity of verbal stimulation received by the typical middle-class child. However, this assumption might also be invalid since certain types of linguistic stimulation may be more important than others in relation to language growth and development. For example, active as opposed to passive dialogue between parent and child is accepted as an extremely important variable insofar as language growth is concerned. Conceivably, the peer group activities and the nurse-child relationship might allow for more active dialogue than occurs in the middle-class home where the mother, in contradistinction, may more frequently read to her child. Which variable is more important? Can the relative importance of the different variables be weighed? Such information is not available at this time; obviously, until such information is obtained, one should be cautious in the interpretation of the verbal environment of the lower-class child. The environment may be as good as or better than the middle-class environment. We simply do not know! There is need for much additional research before this question can be adequately answered. The paradigm in Table 3-1 suggests the kinds of information that should be obtained in order for valid cross-cultural comparisons and analyses to be made.

Table 3-1 Type, Quality, and Quantity of Verbal Interactions

Type	Quality or Kind	Quantity or Amount
Talking to child	May be active or passive;	
Talking to mother	may differ significantly	
Talking to father	dependent upon respondent	The amount of time spent
Talking to peers		in active or passive verbal
Talking to others		interactions needs to be
Reading to child	Usually passive	determined
Telling stories to child		
Singing to child		
TV watching by child		

Significant Sociolinguistic Factors

Origins

Sociolinguistics is the newest in a series of terms used to describe a relatively new field that draws from linguistics, anthropology, and sociology. Basically, it involves systematically studying the relationship between both verbal and nonverbal linguistic forms and social communications; it is concerned with attitudes and opinions and how these judgments are influenced by language transmission systems. In other words, it involves not only what a person says but also how he says it and the effect it has upon the speaker–listener.

The origin of sociolinguistics can be traced to the 1920s and the work of Franz Boas and Edward Sapir, two anthropologists who pioneered the field of social anthropology. Until 1952 the bulk of sociolinguistics consisted of studies of foreign and primitive languages and the characteristics that made the systems different or similar. At that time Hertzler (1965) officially merged linguistics and sociology in a paper read at a meeting of the Midwest Sociological Society, in which he called for more work in the field of the sociology of language. Even though attention was then focused on the sociology of language, "sociolinguistics as an activity specifically directed to an examination of the interaction of language structure and social structure and of the interimplications of speech behavior and social behavior has developed only since the beginning of the sixties" (Grimshaw 1971, p. 93). Labov's remarks made in 1969 still pertain:

> *The study of language change in its social context has been described by some as a virgin field; by others, as a barren territory. A brief examination of what has been written in the past on this subject shows that it is more like an abandoned back yard, overgrown with various kinds of tangled, secondary scholarship. The subject has been so badly treated with voluminous, vacuous, and misleading essays that one can sympathize with linguists who say that it is better left alone . . . . We are then left with such a limited body of fact that we are condemned to repeat the arguments of our predecessors; we find ourselves disputing endlessly about bad data instead of profiting from the rich production of new linguistic change around us. [Labov 1972, p. 260]*

Ethnography and Dialect*

The heart of sociolinguistic investigation invariably centers around and involves some description of ethnography and dialect. Ethnography is the process of con-

---

*An excellent reference to ethnography and communication may be found in the *Journal of Childhood Communication Disorders*, 1(13), 1990 in which the entire journal is devoted to this topic. Also, see *Ethnotes*, a newsletter for professionals interested in studying communication disorders from an ethnographic perspective. The newsletter can be obtained from Joan Good Erickson, 901 South Sixth Street, Champaign, IL 61820.

structing, through direct personal observation of social behavior, a theory of the workings of a particular culture. Because every culture is unique in its views and goals, ethnography attempts to determine how the members try to control or impose order on their environment, how they view their own speech and language in terms of what is good speech, bad speech, appropriate speech, inappropriate speech, defective speech, and how these views are acquired.

Dialect refers to a variety of language spoken by the members of a given speech community, either geographic or social. A dialect may vary in pronunciation, vocabulary, and grammar from other varieties of the same language. Thus, people united by dialect form a speech community. The members of such a community frequently share interests, values, ambitions, and communication systems. It is very hard to differentiate between where a dialect stops and another language starts, but, basically, dialects are enough like each other to be understood by other speakers of different dialects of the same language. Thus, standard or "network" or "establishment" English and its regional variants are mutually understandable.

Ethnographically, people of different societies think differently about language, value it differently, evaluate it differently, acquire it through different social mechanisms, and use it in different situations. For instance, "among the Araucanions it is an insult to be asked to repeat an answer, . . . a prompt answer from a Toba means he has no time to answer questions, . . . [and] a Wasco prefers not to answer a question on the day of its asking" (Hymes 1971, p. 75).

Dialectal Differences

Although only three major dialects are usually recognized in the United States, sociolinguists recognize at least two others in the form of Appalachian and African–American English dialects. Appalachian dialects are but a series of subcultural dialects that are similar enough to be included in one category.

The other major dialect is commonly labeled "black English," or black vernacular (BEV), ebonics, or more currently, African–American English. It is also a cohesive linguistic system that is substantially yet subtly different from standard American English dialects. It is spoken by some African–Americans, particularly those of the lower socioeconomic classes.* When analyzing African–American speaking behaviors,

---

*In order to make a valid determination of the different varieties of black English or Appalachian dialect that may be spoken by speakers of these dialects, it is important that the varied educational, occupational, income, and age groups, i.e., the different socioeconomic, sociopsychological, and other demographic factors, contribute to a language data base. Only in this way can an accurate picture be obtained of these varied dialects. And such data bases can best be obtained through an analysis of the speech patterns of speakers from different environments. To date many of the studies have analyzed the speech patterns of informants from restricted environments. As Williams (1976) points out in his excellent article, "The Anguish of Definition: Toward a New Concept of Blackness," "the lect that one speaks has nothing to do with race but everything to do with social environment" (p. 24).

Bauman (1971, p. 336) described several key acts and events, including rapping, capping, playing the dozens, signifying, shucking, rifting, louding, loud talking, marking, toasting, gaming, and others. How many European–Americans know what these are? Yet, to many African–Americans, they are the most important speech activities in which one can engage. Good talking form then means proficiency in these activities, not talking like English teachers.

African–American dialect, according to some linguists, unlike mountain or Appalachian dialect has a different origin from standard English. Most sociolinguists maintain that present day African–American dialects are derived, not from British dialects as dialectologists have assume, but from a Creole variety of English that was spoken by the earliest slaves. A Creole language is the permanent and primary language form of pidgin. Since pidgin languages are developed to meet a communication emergency, Creole is then a secondary, derived language. As future generations acquire this language, it becomes their primary language. Thus, Creole is a pidgin language made permanent.

Dialect Speech Communities

It is common knowledge that there are dialects unique to subcultures, but few are aware that some commonalities are shared by the various dialectal communities. One of the commonalities involves diglossia (dialect switching, code switching, or bidialectalism), an ability to switch from peer language to standard language. Diglossia is most evident in grammar and vocabulary. Much less frequently can dialect switching be done with phonology. Lexical and syntactic items are apparently more amenable to diglosic self-alterations than phonological ones. Yet these pronunciations most clearly label the dialectal community of the speaker. It is clear, therefore, that additional stress needs to be placed on the achievement of phonological diglossia than perhaps has theretofore been suspected.

Our schools have traditionally worked to eliminate what is properly thought of as uneducated or folk speech, and, in particular, certain kinds of grammatical usage received much attention. For example, the verb agreement (e.g., they is) and the use of adjectival forms for adverbial forms (e.g., he talks good) are considered substandard speech forms in our schools. Little attention has been paid, however, to the intersections of grammar and phonology. Such relationships need to be carefully evaluated. If a speaker or writer regularly drops a final consonant in certain clusters (e.g., omission of final [t] in clusters), the past tense may be lost (e.g., walked becomes walk). If the final [s] is dropped (e.g., two pound), the traditional method of pluralizing words may be altered. Thus, the grammatical consequences of phonological differences need to receive attention, especially as they relate to articulation testing.

Some grammatical differences are socially detrimental and give rise, too frequently, to poor expectations insofar as progress is concerned (Rosenthal effect). Of particular importance is the apparent fact that these kinds of variants cause relatively less immediate damage to the communication process between speaker and auditor than do lexical differences.

Social Implications of Dialectal Speech Patterns

Value judgments are too often the basis for ranking the differences that exist among humankind. In this country, the values, mores, and behaviors, including linguistic behavior, of the middle-class essentially white establishment is accepted as the norm in most cases and, therefore, that which is desirable. Thus, this class's speech pattern is the "standard." As we have alluded to elsewhere, however, all dialects should be considered nonstandard, including the so-called standard dialect; to do otherwise is to perpetuate an ethnocentric value system that ranks the different dialects on a scale ranging from positive to negative.

The social problems or benefits that dialectally distinctive phonological, syntactical, and lexical features may create are not difficult to predict. If one wants to communicate effectively and, at the same time, appeal to certain subcultural groups in our country, one might indicate an awareness of the dialect difference by trying to converse with them in their own dialects. This thesis is not new; politicians and others attempt to generate such communication each time they interact with members of different cultural groups.*

Thus, dialectal speech patterns can be of much benefit to their users, and to surrender such a potential advantage is clearly unwise. Yet much pressure is exerted in our schools and clinics to eliminate differences in speech and language patterns. What is good for the politician, however, may also be desirable for the teacher. To communicate effectively with students is the sine qua non of good teaching, and such communication occurs only when all parties concerned in a verbal interchange clearly understand the denotative and connotative aspects of the interchange. Rather than attempting to eliminate the various dialectal patterns by labeling them substandard, the teacher and clinician should try to learn them and to use them. Such utilization, among other gains, should foster better social acceptance of the teacher and clinician by the child. It should be clearly understood however, that we do not advocate the acceptance of dialectal patterns as the "finished product." Rather, we stress the need for the child, and when possible the teacher, to become a diglossic speaker.

The Interrelation Between Regional and Sociocultural Dialects

From a synchronic point of view, languages may vary both regionally and socially. Regional dialects are those varieties of a language that are distributed geographically, while cultural or social dialects are varieties that are distributed along any of a number of social-scale values (e.g., income, education, and occupation, as well as subcultural membership, and perhaps racial or ethnic group. It would be a mistake to assume that regional and cultural dialects exist independent of each other, for that which is a regional feature in one area may be socially significant in another. In fact, the relation-

---

*For example, Martin Luther King, Jr., was well known for his dialogue skills.

ships between regional and cultural dialects are so complex that such dialects as "standard English," "mountain English," and "African–American English" are meaningless unless considered in relation to regional varieties of American English.

The fact that what is "standard" in one part of the country is different in another sometimes creates problems. Language differences may cast doubt on one's cultural and educational credentials. For example, Southern children who spoke perfectly standard Southern English were often put in speech-correction classes when they moved to cities in the North. Usually, however, the various regional standards are accepted and respected; for that reason Presidents Kennedy (New England), Johnson (Southwest Texas), or Carter (Southeast Georgia) were not hindered politically by their speech. It is because the regional standards vary for the most part in vocabulary and pronunciation that they are generally accepted and respected. There are, however, social class varieties of the regional dialects that stigmatize speakers; they stigmatize the speaker because they differ grammatically.

Clearly, then, cultural or social dialects must be studied within their regional contexts. What is "standard" varies from region to region; so does what is "nonstandard." Just as standard English varies geographically, so do the various cultural dialects. Thus it is doubtful that there is a monolithic black English or mountain English; rather there are probably black Englishes and mountain Englishes. No account of language variation is complete unless both the horizontal and vertical dimensions are studied.

There is a direct interrelationship of dialect to one's social status and to geographic region of residence. Thus, a speaker of African–American English who is lower class and lives in Watts (Los Angeles) will manifest differences in this dialect as compared to a middle-class African–American who also lives in Watts as well as to another lower-class speaker who lives in Knoxville. Similarly, the speaker of standard (network or establishment) English will speak different dialects dependent upon his or her social status (middle vs. lower class) and geographical residence (e.g., Boston or Atlanta).

Similarities as well as differences in dialect are found as a function of social class and race. For example, lower-lower class African–American and white speakers possess many similarities in their speech patterns as well as some notable differences. Similarly upper-middle class black, Hispanic, or Appalachian speakers, for example, may manifest some slight differences in prosody if their sociocultural environments were characterized by segregated schooling. But the similarities far outweigh the differences that may be present. The same patterns exist between middle- and lower-class African–American speakers or Hispanic speakers; that is, there are similarities as well as differences in their varied speech patterns. The determining factor is, as noted above, the sociocultural environment in which the children are reared. When the children are exposed to integrated communities, they learn to use dialectal forms representative of the different speech models inherent to the community. Chapter 4 discusses these differences in much detail. Some common examples of African-influenced English and Appalachian-influenced English are as follows:

Some Specifics of African–American Dialect

1. Absence of copula verb
2. No distinction in gender for third-person plural pronoun
3. Distinction between second-person singular and plural
4. Prefixing or suffixing third-person plural objective case pronouns for noun pluralization
5. No obligatory plural morpheme
6. No obligatory third-person singular marker for verbs
7. No obligatory possessive marker
8. Use of specific phrases to announce beginnings of sentences
9. Use of intonational ranges to mark meaning differences

Some Specifics of Appalachian English

1. A verb*ing* (a-hunting)
2. Double modals (might could)
3. Completive done (done finished)
4. Invariant *be*
5. *s* form in third plural of verbs (some people makes it)
6. Irregular plural forms in nouns (waspes; waspers)
7. Expletive they and it (They's catfish in the river)
8. Plural possessives with –*n* (yourn)
9. Irregular relative pronouns (he's the man what did it)
10. Positive anymore (he lives here anymore)

A word of caution is in order for the student of mountain English. First, the various Appalachian dialects have been largely ignored; further study may alter the descriptions given here. Second, as has been shown in this section, the study of regional dialects without consideration of their social implications or the study of cultural–social dialects out of their regional context is meaningless.

4

Language Patterns of Nonstandard Speakers

African–American Linguistic System

Most Common Linguistic Variants

Deletion of plural and possessive forms of *s* is used for the third-person singular form of present tense verbs; the irregular verbs change pronunciation instead of omitting the final *s*. As Wolfram and Fasold (1974) cite, in black English, "has" is pronounced as have (not ha'); "does" becomes "do" (not doe'); and "says" is "say" (not se). Also the vowel sounds are distorted in other verbs, such as with cases of past tense and past participles; examples are "tell–told" becomes "tol'"; "leave–left" becomes "lef'"; and "sleep–slept" is "slep'." In summary, the obvious phonological endings are absent in the past tense forms, yet the underlying linguistic concept of tensing is intact. This conclusion, however, is not valid for the actual omitted *s*, which constitutes an error in grammatical constructions.

Black English has the tendency to omit the medial *r*. When the omission occurs, a listener interprets it as a "lost" syllable. Examples such as "sto'y" (story), "ma'y" (marry), and "te'ific" (terrific) could lead to misunderstandings in meaning. Usually this phenomenon happens when the *r* follows a vowel and precedes another vowel in the same word (see previous examples). Frequently the deleted *r* occurs in the final

---

Note that research by Dr. William Labov, as reported in *The New York Times* (March 15, 1985), has allowed him to conclude that the form of English spoken by many black Americans is becoming more different from standard English rather than more like it.

position of a word (e.g., "ca'" for "car"). Perhaps blending and/or balancing aspects are being enforced (Wolfram and Fasold 1974, pp. 140–141).

The addition of the perfect structure of "done" is found within the phonological character of black speech. "Done" is utilized as a means of emphasis or as a "completeness of the action." Today, evidence indicates the use of "done" is on the decline (Wolfram and Fasold 1974, p. 142). For example: "I done told you to stop that!"

One unique characteristic of the black dialect is the deleted forms of contrasted auxiliaries. At times entire words are left out. The following examples illustrate this point:

"I done that lots of times."	(deletion and contraction of "have")
"He go there tomorrow."	(deletion and contraction of "will")
"They over there all the time."	(deletion and contraction of "are" or "is")

It has been postulated that the contractions are used because the missing words (have, will, are/is) have lost their distinctiveness in the sentence structure. It is believed that the difference between past tense and the past participle are not necessary to the black speaker who does not generalize these forms over to the past tense forms.

Finally, one of the most documented "nonstandard" usages found in the literature is the use of "be" to denote a temporal action or as an object or event distributed intermittently in time (see Wolfram and Fasold 1974, p. 161). Standard English speakers consider "be" to be a form of "am," "is," and "are," but black English uses the form quite differently. "Be" can appear in three meaningful contexts:

1. "If somebody hit him, Darryl 'be' mad."
   Explanation: Future reaction to being hit with the deletion of "will" or the contracted form of "will."
2. "If somebody hit him, Darryl 'be' mad."
   Explanation: Probability of being hit with the deletion of "would be" or the contracted form of "d."
3. "If somebody hit him, Darryl "be" mad."
   Explanation: Statement of Darryl's habitual reaction of being hit, with this form occurring most frequently.

Phonological Differences

Word–Final Consonant Clusters Standard English words ending in a consonant cluster or blend often have the final member of the cluster absent in black English. In black English, words such as "test" and "desk" are pronounced as "tes'" and "des'." Because of this, we find that pairs of words such as "build" and "bill" have identical pronunciations in black English. It is important to distinguish two basic types of clusters that are affected by this sort of reduction. First, clusters in which both members of the cluster belong to the same "base word" can be reduced, as in "tes'" and "des'." Reduction also affects final *t* or *d*, which results when the suffix *–ed* is added to the base word. In black English, when the addition of the *–ed* suffix results in either a voiced or voiceless cluster, the cluster may be reduced by removing the final member of the cluster. This affects *–ed* when it functions as a past tense marker, a participle, or an adjective, although its association with the past tense is the most frequent.

Related to the reduction of final consonant clusters in black English is a particular pattern of pluralization involving the *–s* and *–es* plural forms. In black English words ending in *s* plus *p*, *t*, or *k* add the *–es* plural instead of the *–s* plural. Thus, words like "desk" or "ghost" are pluralized as "deses" and "ghoses." It is essential to understand that this is a *regular* pluralization pattern due to the status of final consonant clusters in black English.

th Sounds   In black English the regular pronunciation rules for the sounds represented by *th* are quite different from standard English. The particular sounds that *th* represents are mainly dependent on the context in which *th* occurs. At the beginning of a word the *th* is frequently pronounced as a *d* in black English, so words such as "the" and "that" are pronounced as "de" and "dat." In the case of the voiceless *th* in words such as "thought" and "think," *th* is sometimes pronounced as *t*; thus these words are pronounced as "tought" and "tink." In the middle of the word there are several different pronunciations for *th* in black English. For the voiceless sound as in "nothing," most frequently it is pronounced as *f*, thus pronounced as "nuf-n." For the voiced sound as in "brother," most frequently it is pronounced as *v*, thus pronounced as "bruvah." At the end of a word *f* is the predominant pronunciation of *th* in words such as "tooth" and "south," which are pronounced as "toof" and "souf."

r and l   At the beginning of a word, *r* and *l* are always pronounced. The most important context to recognize is the so-called loss of *r* and *l* when they follow a vowel. In such items as "steal" and "bear" a reduction of *r* and *l* will be pronounced alike. There is also a tendency to drop the *l*; thus "toll" and "toe" would be pronounced alike. The *r* absence is occasionally observed between two vowels within a word. Thus, it is possible to get "Ca'ol" and "sto'y" for "Carol" and "story."

Final b, d, g   At the end of a syllable the voiced stops *b*, *d*, and *g* are often pronounced as the corresponding voiceless stops, *p*, *t*, and *k*, respectively. In addition to the devoicing rule, some speakers may have the complete absence of the stop *d*. This results in pronunciation such as "goo'man." The rule for the absence of *d* occurs more frequently when *d* is followed by a consonant than when followed by a vowel.

Indefinite Articles a and an   In black English, as in some varieties of white Southern speech, the article "a" is used regardless of how the following word begins. With a selected group of words that may begin with a vowel similar to *a* (phonetically ə), the article may also be completely absent or at least "merge" together, thus resulting in "he had eraser."

Grammatical Differences

Verbs and Auxiliaries   Differences in verb agreement are among the most frequently reported aspects of black English. The third-person singular has no obligatory morphological ending in nonstandard English, so that "she works hard" becomes "she work hard." Subject–verb agreement may also differ in black English; thus, the black speaker may say "She have bike" or "They was going." The use of the copula is not obligatory in black English: "I going," "He a bad boy." Nonstandard usage of verb tense among black speakers has also been reported. The black speaker may use "drunk" for "drank" and "walk" for "walked." Irregular tenses are marked by black speakers, but the regular *–ed* is not; "done" is utilized with the past tense of the verb to indicate completed action. There is also nonstandard usage of future tenses by black speakers: "I will go home" becomes "I'ma go." The African–American dialect has an unmarked form of the verb which is noncommittal as to time orientation, although there are certain forms that are past future respectively. It appears that "was" is reserved for events that are completely in the past, while "been" extends from the past up to, and even including, the present moment. "Be" is a simple future, with "gonna" the intentional future.

The omission of auxiliary verbs is common among black English speakers: "He been here." Wolfram and Fasold (1974) report that speakers of nonstandard English omit auxiliaries in questions using "what, when, and where": "What you want?" In standard English the present progressive is marked in two ways: "He is going" contains the auxiliary "be" and affix *–ing.* In black English only the second element is necessary: "He going home." In the so-called present perfect, "I have lived here" is the standard English form, whereas either "I have live here" or "I have lived here" is permissible in black English. Black English exhibits the use of the uninflected form of "be" to indicate habitual or general state: "He be workin'" means that he generally works. In contrast, "he workin'" can simply mean that he is working at this moment.

–s Suffixes   Black English indicates possessive by the order of the words. The phrase "the boy hat" corresponds to "the boy's hat" in standard English. When the second noun is deleted, the black English form does mark the possessive with *'s.* "This is John's" is the possessive, whereas "This is John" has a quite different meaning. The *–s* (or *–es*) suffixes that mark most plurals in standard English are occasionally absent in black English. This results in sentences like "He took five book." Black English speakers tend to omit the obligatory morphemes of the plural when numerical quantifiers such as two, seven, or nine are used: "nine cent," "two foot." Black English speakers may add the plural suffix *–s* to forms which in standard English have irregular forms: "mans."

Pronouns A well-known, but little understood, feature of nonstandard English dialects, including black English, is pronominal apposition. Pronominal apposition is the construction used in apposition to the noun subject of the sentence. Usually the nominative form of the pronoun is used as in "My brother, he bigger than you." Occasionally, the objective or possessive pronoun is used in apposition as well, as in "That girl name Wanda, I never did like her." Where standard English uses "there" in an existential or expletive function, black English uses "it." This results in sentences like "It's a boy in my room name Robert"; standard English would have been "There's a boy in my room named Robert." Bailey (1965) states that the form "they" replaces the possessive pronoun "their" in black English: "Everybody look down at they feet."

Adjectives Loban (1966) reports the nonstandard modification of adjectives in black English: "That girl is more pretty than the other one."

Adverbs Loban (1966) also reports the nonstandard modification of adverbs in black English: "I guess he arrived quick." The formal *–ly* adverb marker is not used in black English.

Prepositions Baratz (1969) points out the substitution of the preposition "to" for "at" in black English: "He over to his friend's house." Labov (1966) reports the use of "upside" for "in" in the speech of 17-year-old black boys: "Hit him upside the head."

Negation Negation is a feature that is marked twice in black English and once in standard English. A standard English speaker might say "Didn't anybody see it?" and a black English speaker might say "Didn't nobody see it?" Baratz (1969) reports an unusual usage of "ain't" and "don't" by American black speakers. "Ain't" is used consistently in nonverbal predications and before the tense markers; it also seems to be the form preferred before the progressive *–in* form of the verb. Whether this exhausts its limitations, and whether "don't" is used in other cases, remains to be investigated. Examples of the use of "don't" and "ain't" are "I ain't paying that kind of bread for no iron like that" and "I don't know why he done it." Table 4-1 presents a translation from standard English to black English which incorporates many of the previously noted dialect forms.

Mountain (Appalachian) Linguistic System

Most Common Mountain Variants

In Appalachian English the *r* is deleted in either of two cases: (1) after a vowel and (2) as a final consonant. The listener immediately picks up the *r* deletion in pronouns such as "their" and "your," which become "they" and "you" in Appalachian speech.

A very common aspect of Appalachian English—present progressive forms of certain American verbs and some past tense/nonpast tense verb forms—has been extensively

Table 4-1 A Translation from Standard to Black English Dialect

1. It was a man named Nicodemus. He was a leader of the Jews.

2. This man, he come to Jesus in the night and say, "Rabbi, we know you a teacher that come from God, cause can't nobody do the things you be doing 'cept he got God with him."

3. Jesus he tell him say, "This ain't no jive, if a man ain't born over again, ain't no way he gonna get to know God."

4. Then Nicodemus, he ask him, say "How a man gonna be born when he already old? Can't nobody go back inside his mother and get born."

5. So Jesus tell him, say, "This ain't no jive, this the truth. The onliest way a man gonna get to know God, he got to get born regular and he got to get born from the Holy Spirit."

6. The body can only make a body get born, but the spirit, he make a man so he can get God.

7. Don't be surprised just cause I tell you that you got to get born over again.

8. The wind blow where it want to blow and you can't hardly tell where it's coming from and where it's going to. That's how it go when somebody get born over again by the Spirit.

9. So Nicodemus say, "How you know that?"

10. Jesus say, "You call yourself a teacher that teach Israel and you don't know these kinds of things?"

11. I'm gonna tell you, we talking about something we know about cause we already seen it. We telling it like it is and you-all think we jiving and don't believe me, what's gonna happen when I tell you about things you can't see?

12. Ain't nobody gone up to Heaven 'cept Jesus, who come down from Heaven.

13. Just like Moses done hung up the shake in the wilderness, Jesus got to be hung up.

14. So that peoples believe in him, he can give them real life that ain't never gonna end.

15. God really did love everybody in the world. In fact, he loved the people so much that he done gave up the onliest son he had. Any man that believe in Him, he gonna have a life that ain't never gonna end. He ain't never gonna die. God, he didn't send His Son to the world to act like a judge, but He sent Him to rescue the peoples in the world.

Source: From W.A. Wolfram and Ralph W. Fasold, "Toward Reading Materials for Speakers of Black English: Three Linguistically Appropriate Passages," in J.C. Baratz and R.W. Shuy (eds.), *Teaching Black Children to Read* (Arlington, VA: Center for Applied Linguistics, 1969), pp. 150–151. Reprinted by permission.

studied by Wolfram and Christian (1975). The *a* as a prefix is added to the verb + *ing* construction; however, the *g* is omitted. Thus, *a* + verb + *in* is the final product.

Common verbs in mountain English are "come, go, take off." They function as adverbial complements or as verbs to represent continuing or initial action—that is, "keep, start, and stay, get to, pull, cry, want."

The *a*–prefixing constructions are not used on verbs acting as gerunds. Wolfram and his colleagues did not find this unique structure following the prepositions "on" and "at." In other words, when two prepositions are used together, the speaker will not use the *a*–prefixing form. This, though, is true in standard English since standard grammatical construction does not allow the pronunciation of two successive prepositions. Another rule associated with *a*–prefixing deals with stressing. The form is not used before verbs initiated by an unstressed syllable. Two unstressed syllables usually do not occur in succession. As with the case of two prepositions, two unstressed syllables are rare in standard English usage. These two examples further strengthen the argument in favor of nonstandard dialects as being bona fide entities; they should not be considered any less complex or functional than standard English.

The phonological constraints on *a*–prefixing can be summarized as follows (Wolfram and Christian 1975, pp. 254–261):

1. Not observed when following a morpheme beginning with a vowel
    Example: "John was a-eatin' his food."
2. Avoided by moving it to the preceding auxiliary
    Example: "The movie was a-shockin'."
3. Appears more on stressed initial syllables
    Examples: "a-struttin' and a-draggin'" (Construction does not appear in *a*–prefixing.)
4. Deletion of *a* favored when the word preceding *a*–prefixing is a vowel
    Example: "John is eating his food."

During a lecture given at the University of Tennessee in 1977, Wolfram cited some other possible phonological constraints: The Appalachian English speakers do not use the *s* as many black English speakers do. The *s* is now weak in mountain English, and its use is not generalized to other verbs, such as go, goes. Appalachian speech is fairly consistent in using *s* in its commonly acceptable form on third-person singular constructions.

Pluralization and possessive irregularities are not as predominant in Appalachian English as they are in black English. Most examples linguists have found pertaining to pluralization consist of adding the plural forms to irregular nouns. Some rural mountain speakers will use "feets" for feet; "childrens" (chillerns) for children; and "peoples" for people. Omissions are frequently found on four "mile," five "apple," or three "pound."

The possessive *s* forms are used fairly consistently with the accepted standard forms. One unique possessive form is indicated by the use of *n* on pronouns. Words such as "yourn, hisn, hern, ourn, theirn" have been noted. Oddly enough the root of this peculiar form stems from an Old English form found in the south and Midlands of England. The use of *n* or *en* was noted when the pronoun occurs in an absolute position, such as, "It's yourn," but not when modifying a preceding noun phrase, as with "It's yourn house." This form is dying out quickly, being replaced by the appropriate use of the possessive *s* (Wolfram and Christian 1975).

The use of "ain't" is extremely common in the nonstandard dialects of the United States. It has been found in the dialects of African–Americans along the Atlantic

Coast (Labov 1966), with Puerto Rican speakers (Wolfram and Fasold 1971), and in Appalachia (Wolfram and Christian 1975). "Ain't" is a form used to denote a negative function. Two rules exist for its use within the realms of nonstandard English:

> *For emphasis, incorporate a copy of the NOT which is in the main verb phrase in "all" indefinites after the main verb phrase, but leave the original NOT intact; (2) for emphasis, incorporate a "copy" of the NOT which is in the main verb phrase or the preverbal indefinite into the main verb phrase (if it is not there already) and in "all" indefinites after the main verb phrase, but leave the original NOT intact. [Wolfram and Fasold 1974, pp. 163–164]*

The use of double or multiple negatives, such as "He don't know nothing," is a common negative construction in the Appalachian dialect. It can be used for emphasis and does not follow the convention that two negatives make a positive. Actually, the double negatives express the intended meaning of the sentence with the second negative acting as a "copy" of the first negative.

So, as with the discussion of black English, many linguistic and phonological differences exist between Appalachian English and standard English. The differences are not to be construed as the ignorant verbalizations of rural farmers. Appalachian speech has a definite place among standard English utterances and should be considered as equal, not as substandard. The chapter appendix gives additional examples of both African–American (black English) and Appalachian linguistic differences.

Paralinguistics: Body Language and Prosody

Laypersons and professional workers alike often foster the gross misconception that the majority of communication transpires by verbal means. The realm of nonverbal communication, including body language and the prosody of the linguistic system, is of unquestionable importance in the interpretation of a message and its impact upon the auditor. Until recently, scant research has investigated the paralinguistic aspects even within the mainstream culture, much less among different cultures. Such differences among cultures appear to be glaring and may cause profound errors in communication due to ignorance of their significance. It is imperative the clinicians examine in detail all aspects of the communication of their culturally different clients. To understand and to utilize the total linguistic and paralinguistic systems of other cultures is the key to effective communication.

*Body Language**

Nonverbal communication is a silent language that everyone uses day after day, sometimes without awareness. People constantly send and receive nonverbal mes-

---

*See Chapter 3 for additional information.

sages, but very few consider the possibilities that lie within this relatively uncharted field. The way the person decodes these variables dictates his or her interpretation of the people and situations involved. Linguistic symbols and their nonverbal components operate in a synchronized, coordinated way in human communication, and the nonverbal components may be either in accordance with or contradictory to the verbal message. Nonverbal components consist of such things as gesturing, eye contact, a certain distance between individuals, posture, and timing. From a variety of studies it becomes evident that verbal signals have little meaning apart from the specific situation in which they are uttered. Nonverbal modes "fill in the gaps" of communication, especially in emotional attitudinal communication, which is expressed primarily by kinesics and paralanguage. No language response can be separated from the contextual patterning in which it occurs.

Eye Contact   Eye contact behavior is one component that appears to have wide cultural variance. In the white middle-class culture the speaker who does not meet and maintain acceptable eye contact is apt to have his sincerity doubted. When others refuse to meet our eyes when we are speaking, we are likely to suspect disinterest or indifference. In Puerto Rican culture, however, children learn early that to communicate respect one does not maintain eye contact with adults. To refuse to do so is a sign of obedience (Fast 1970). Similarly, Native American children of various cultural tribes in the Southwest, like Puerto Rican children, lower their heads and eyes as a sign of deference when an adult encounters them face to face (Galloway 1970). It has been demonstrated repeatedly that culturally different students who attend inner-city schools are frequently paying attention (e.g., sitting with lowered heads and eyes) when their behavior would seem to indicate otherwise.

Space and Interpersonal Distance   The use of space and desired interpersonal distance also varies considerably. Jews and Italians, for example, have greater preference for physical closeness and touching. Mexican–Americans stand very close together when conversing. Blacks greet each other at a greater personal distance than whites. In Asian cultures crowding together is a sign of warmth and pleasant intimacy (Fast 1970).

Posture and Body Movement   The importance of posture and body movement for communicating varies among cultures. Among black males, postural stance is recognized as an important means of projecting self-image; among Appalachians a guarded and slow-moving movement pattern accompanying a cautious verbal response pattern has been described by Glenn (1970).

Facial Displays   Although facial displays of the primary affects are pancultural, the rules that regulate affect displays are learned and are culture-specific. There is evidence to an instructor's display of positive affect; that is, interaction in a nonverbal manner and conveying much personal warmth may enhance learning significantly in these children (Kleinfield 1973). This may not hold true for African–Americans, however. A study by Hawkes and Middleman (1972) indicated that black children manifested no significant differences on task performance with regard to affect of the teacher.

Prosody or the Suprasegmentals of Language

The speech rhythm that accompanies each linguistic utterance of culturally different speakers is unique. In addition to its recognition value, speech rhythm contributes significantly to the intelligibility of the utterance* as well as to the attitudinal state of the speaker.

Intonational patterns are basic to the vocal code; that is, the variety of inflectional contours and pitch ranges contributes greatly to the differences that occur in cross-cultural communication. For example, the following intonation patterns were found to be characteristic of black English as opposed to standard English: (1) a wider pitch range, extending with high pitch levels, (2) more level and rising final pitch contours, (3) greater use of falling final contours with general yes/no questions in formal and, perhaps, threatening situations, (4) the frequent use of a falsetto or "high" pitch during greetings. In a great many African languages, especially in West Africa, the pitch level is an extremely important component in the communication process. It is thought that this African influence has been transmitted to the current users of black English.

Syllabication and stress are other components of the vocal code that may differ. African–American speakers commonly stress the first syllable of bisyllabic words, while standard speakers will generally stress the last syllable.

It is obviously important that the teacher or clinician be familiar with the various codes of his or her students; to do otherwise is to risk potentially disastrous communication breakdowns. For example, it would be inappropriate if a clinician thought the habitually and culturally proper soft voice of an Asian child was pathological and so attempted to treat it. Likewise, attempting to alter a black child's use of a falling final intonation when asking a question may be improper. But the teacher, unaware of this pattern, might be upset when a child says "You the teacher?" with a falling inflection—such a pattern might well be considered rude or demanding. Further, if teachers or clinicians have little knowledge of the nonverbal language of students or patients, they are likely to impose and project their own code on a child, which could cause an increasing withdrawal pattern and alienation of a child. Table 4-2 gives examples of different prosodic features as a function of cultural membership, whereas Table 4-3 shows the prosody inherent to black English.

---

*As a member of the Ohio State University Psycholinguistic Laboratory team that developed the international alphabet of the air: alpha, bravo, charlie, etc., the author noted that the use of emotion in one's voice contributed significantly to the intelligibility of the message being transmitted.

Table 4-2 Paralanguage: Some Examples of the Different Prosodic Features as a Function of Cultural Membership

	Blacks	Middle-Class Whites	Appalachians
Pitch	Falsetto used often; wider pitch range	Increase of pitch in excitement	Monotonous and emotionless
Loudness	Often quite loud	Range from soft in intimate to loud in anger situations	At same level most of the time
Inflection	Falling final contours	Raise final contours in questions	Flat, monotonous; inflection usage is rare; monosyllabic responses
Timing	Pause and increased pitch to indicate continuation; rhythmic	Rapid-fire verbalization	Slow and deliberate with much pause and spacing

Table 4-3 Prosodic Features of the Black English Dialect

intensity	∧ —loud ∨ —soft	pitch	↑ high ↓ low	tempo	> fast < slow

                                                        ∧ ∧ ∨∨
Well, I grew up in, ah, a canary-colored house, trimmed in white, on a corner, a

↓   ↓   ↓ ∧ ∧   ↓ ↓
hundred fifty lot, hundred by fifty. Trees on each side, rose bushes in front and back, and

                     > ∧ ∧   ∧ ∧
honeysuckle which I used to have to work, mow the lawn, take care of the flowers, which

         ∧ ∧ ∨ ∨   < < > >
I never did mind, as a kid. And I lived in a neighborhood where I was the only Negro. I

              ∨   ∨   ∧ ∧ ∨∨
didn't understand my people when I come here. Ah, they was different. I didn't

          ∧ ∧   ∨ ∨ ∧∧ ∨
understand this ridiculing, criticizing one another.

Source: From R. McDavid and W. Austin, *Communication Barriers to the Culturally Deprived* (Washington, D.C.: USDE Cooperative Research Project 2107, 1966).

The Interrelation of Linguistic Symbols, Body Language, and Prosody

Psychologist Albert Mehrabian (1969) has devised a formula that he feels reveals how much each of the three communicative components (the linguistic code and the two paralinguistic attributes) contribute to the effect the message has upon the receiver. He indicates that the verbal portion of the message is responsible for 7% of the total impact of the message, the prosodic or suprasegmental portion, 38%, and facial expression, a facet of body language, 55% (see Figure 4-1). Thus, in face-to-face interactions people rely much more on prosodic and facial cues than on verbal content in determining another's attitude toward them. Thus, the importance of the nonlinguistic components is expressed primarily by means of paralanguage and not by language per se.

It is clearly incumbent upon the clinician to try to recognize and understand these paralinguistic concomitants if effective communication with the client is to occur. The average person, unschooled in cultural codes of body language, often misinterprets what he or she sees. Since differences between cultures appear to be pronounced in the area of nonverbal behavior, it is desirable that we learn to recognize these culture-specific differences.

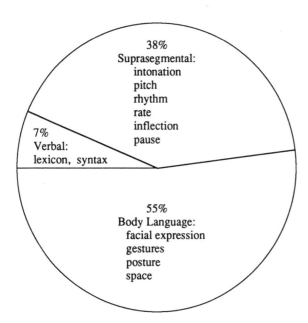

Figure 4-1 Components Contributing to the Total Impact of a Communicated Message (Based on findings of Mehrabian 1969.)

Implications of Culture-Specific Behaviors for Cross-Cultural Communication

Kochman (1971) presents an intriguing analysis of communication failure. He suggests that it is the conflicting nonverbal messages that are primarily responsible when there is a breakdown of cross-cultural communication. He maintains that people fail to communicate because they do not adequately read the cultural signs that each person is sending. This failure consistently produces anger, bewilderment, frustration, and pain. Communication becomes virtually impossible when people not only operate from different codes, but also are unaware that different codes are in operation. Invariably, it has been the minority or subordinate cultural groups in society that suffer when communication fails.

Culture-Specific Behaviors and the Clinician-Child interaction

It is obviously desirable that the clinician be familiar with the cultural background of the client, not only to allow for correct diagnosis as to "deficiency" or "difference" in the child's linguistic patterns, but to avoid misinterpretation of the child's culturally determined paralinguistic behaviors. For example, if the clinician assumed the eye contact behaviors of the Hispanic or black child indicated inattention or disrespect, it would probably alter the clinician's relationship with the child and would definitely give the clinician a false impression regarding the child's motivation. Furthermore, according to Tarone (1972), black children often "compete" verbally; this causes an element of aggressiveness and competitiveness in their communication which may be interpreted as hostility and would alter the relationship with the client.

Suggestions for Altering Possible Detrimental Nonverbal Behaviors

Goals for an instructional unit in nonverbal communication for students and teachers may include the following:

1. Learning to express one's own reactions more freely and accurately and recognizing how members of other cultures use nonverbal behavior to communicate
2. Gaining an understanding of how spacing affects communication and that what constitutes negative violation of space varies from culture to culture
3. Understanding effects of territory communication (Note that the physical environment in which therapy takes place may be communicating so much formality to the child that verbal responses are stifled.)
4. Gaining an understanding of the role of posture and bodily movement in communication (Note that the way a child sits or stands can be an important cue to his receptivity to the therapy that is being presented.)

This kind of training, as well as training in other related areas, should be given to all SLSs and educators. We believe that students need to be able to recognize and understand these culturally specific behavior patterns.

Table 4-4 depicts some kinesic differences evident in common situations between black, particularly black lower-class speakers, and members of the middle class. Note, in particular, the style manifested during a job interview; undoubtedly such behavior "turns off" the middle-class employer. Similarly, the behavior pattern manifested in school would tend to alienate most teachers who are unaware of these cultural differences.

Table 4-4 Kinesic Differences in Everyday Situations

	Black Lower Class	Middle Class
Job interview situation (first impressions)		
Distance	Greets people at greater distances.	
Eye contact	Reluctant to gain eye contact, which is a nonverbal pattern in West African cultures. This pattern is a way of communicating recognition of an authority subordinate relationship.	Direct eye contact communicates trustworthiness and sincerity.
Speaker–listener relationship	Will look away from another while listening and at him while speaking.	Opposite
Vocal activity interactions	The conversation between black lower-class and middle-class people may lack a rhythmic interactional pattern.	
Perception of space	Requires less personal space.	Requires more personal space.
Walking situation	Slow walk with head elevated and tipped to the side; one arm swings with hand slightly cupped. The gait is slow and rhythmic, almost like a walking dance, and is called a "pimp strut."	Brisk walk, characterized by walking on the balls of one's feet with strides of presumed authority; both arms will swing.
School situation (teacher-pupil misunderstanding)		
Reprimand/lecture response of "rolling the eyes"	Communicates general disapproval and/or hostility to the person in the authority role. Eyes are moved from one side of eyesocket to the other side in a low arc, an action that is witnessed more often in females.	

Table 4-4 *Continued*

	Black Lower Class	Middle Class
Greetings (to friends and to people trusted)		
Touching		Salutation and a hug or kiss.
"Cutting the eyes"		Eye movement toward rather than away from another person, immediately followed by a stare.
Body stance	Assumes a "limp stance" becoming an object—no longer a person; often misread as indicating disinterest.	Assumes a stiff position—hands clamped to sides.
"Walk away"	Determines how well a reprimand has been received (e.g., if "pimp strut" used in walking away from the scene, displaying discipline is usually useless).	
Distance/space	Requires more closeness from the teacher as child requires less personal space.	
Verbal greeting	Will approach another member of his culture, verbally greet him, and then may turn his back on him, which requires putting oneself in a vulnerable position relative to one's physical safety and thus indicates an acceptance of the other person.	
Group gatherings (street corners and pool halls)		
Movement	Moves constantly in and out from the center of the circle and assumes a stationary "pimp strut," dancing in place and practicing competitive words games. Stands with hands halfway in pockets; the free arm will swing, point, and gesture to emphasize conversation.	Remains stationary in the circle.

Table 4-4 *Continued*

	Black Lower Class	Middle Class
Conversation	"Sounding," "dozens," and "one liners" are competitive games played by adolescents; older members of a gang participate in "toasts" or poems recited on street corners or in hang-outs. They are spoken with special voice quality and rhythm. *How* one says something is much more important than *what* one says.	
Religious situations	In a black sermon the trials of life are cast into a rhythmic mold.	
Male/Female relationships		
"Stances"	"Rapping stance" or stationary "pimp strut" assumed when a young male talks romantically to a female.	

Chapter 4 Appendix

Phonological, Syntactical, and Lexical Contrasts in Black English and Appalachian English Dialects

	Phonological Differences: Black Dialect	
	Standard English	Dialect
Consonant omissions		
r phoneme	car	ca
l phoneme	tool	too
s phoneme (indicating pluralization)	past	pass
Simplification of consonant clusters	meant	men
	hold	hole
	bowel	bo
Vowel and diphthong alterations		
Short and long o usually made without distinctions	caught	cot
Vowels not distinguished		
Before r	bare	bar
Before l	all	oil
Before nasals	pin	pen
Prevalent substitutions		
f for θ	Ruth	roof
v for δ	bathe	bave

	Phonological Differences: Appalachian Dialect	
	Standard English	Dialect
Consonant omissions		
Initial unstressed syllable sounds	across	'crost
	account	'count
	appears	'pears
Two stop sounds	directly	direckly
	exactly	exackly
	children	chillern
d or t	let's	less
Medial r	burst	bust
	horse	hoss
	first	fust
Consonant omissions		
t after ep	slept	slep
	kept	kep
	crept	crep
t after f	soft	sof
	loft	lof

Chapter 4 Appendix *Continued*

	Phonological Differences: Appalachian Dialect	
	Standard English	Dialect
t after *s*	just	jus
	Baptist	Baptis
d after *n* and *l*	old	ole
	hand	han
p after *s*	clasp	clas
	wasp	wasper
Consonant additions		
p if consonant is voiceless	comfort	compfort
l when followed by consonant *t* or *d*	miles	milts
	else	elts
Substitutions		
i/e	been	ben
i/a	bring	brang
e/i	get	git
	chest	chist
o/e	window	winder
	hollow	holler
u/i	brush	brish
	such	sich
	just	jist
t/d	salad	salat
d/t	twenty	twendy
k/t	vomit	vomick
ch/t	tune	chune
	Tuesday	Cheusday
dz/d	tedious	tejous

	Syntactical Differences: Black Dialect[*]	
	Standard English	Black Dialect
Linking verb	He is going.	He goin'.
Possessive marker	John's cousin.	John cousin.
Plural marker	I have five cents.	I got five cent.
Subject expression	John lives in New York.	John he live in New York.
Verb form	I drank the milk.	I drunk the milk.
Past marker	Yesterday he walked home.	Yesterday he walk home.
Verb agreement	He runs home.	He run home.
	She has a bicycle.	She have a bicycle.
Future form	I will go home.	I'ma go home.
"If" construction	I asked if he did it.	I ask did he do it.
Negation	I don't have any.	I don't got none.
	He didn't go.	He ain't go.
Indefinite article	I want an apple.	I want a apple.

Chapter 4 Appendix *Continued*

Syntactical Differences: Black Dialect		
	Standard English	Black Dialect
Pronoun form	We have to do it.	Us got to do it.
	His book.	He book.
Preposition	He is over at his friend's house.	He over to his friend house.
	He teaches at Francis Pool.	He teach Francis Pool.
"Be"	Statement: He is here all the time.	Statement: He be here.
"Do"	Contradiction: No, he isn't.	Contradiction: No, he don't.

Syntactical Differences: Appalachian Dialect		
	Standard English	Dialect
Pronoun usage		
Emphatic demonstrative	that	thar
	this	this'n
Disjunctive possessive	his	hisn
	your	yourn
Alteration of reflexive pronouns	himself	hisself
	themselves	thesselves
Other changes or variations	it	hit
	those boys	them boys
Noun usage		
Noun compounds	church	church-house
	Bible	Bible-book
Noun pluralism	posts	postes
	beasts	beastes
Collective sense	seven years ago	seven year back
	six feet tall	six foot high
Adding "er" to noun compounds	new-born	new-born'der
Verbal usage		
Strong preterites	drove	driv
	broke	bruk
	climbed	clum
Weak preterites	knew	knowed
	drew	drawed
	caught	ketched
Addition of *ed* to past tense	born	borned
	cost	costed
Conversion noun to verb	It won't please her.	Hit won't pleasure her.
Pleonasms—redundancies	nap	nap o'sleep
	during	durin' the while
	a small fellow	a little bitty feller
Agreement of subject and verb	he is going	he go
Adding *er*/*est* to form comparative	only	onliest

Chapter 4 Appendix *Continued*

Lexical Differences: Black Dialect

Dialect Word	Standard English Equivalent
†rapping	colorful rundown of a past event
jiving or shucking	speech used when talking to a representative of the establishment, the "man"
rundown	narration of a past event
†bread or cakes	money
wheels	car
headbreakers	policement
whips	white power structure (acronym)
scuffler	one who barely gets by from day to day engaging in such nonprestigious activities as begging, working at odd jobs at minimum wages, collecting and returning pop bottles for deposit, etc.
†drag	something not enjoyed
†hung-up	problem
†put-down	victimized by another person
strung out	victimized by heroin
nose open	victimized by love
broom	fast getaway

Lexical Differences: Appalachian Dialect

Dialect Word	Standard English Equivalent
stout	good health
pack	carry
sorry	inferior
heap	much
poke	small bag
bealed ear	running ear
larripin	very good
meetin'	church
peaked	sick-looking
'pears	seems
tuckered out	tired
wrench	rinse
spigot	faucet
carry (me to town)	take (me to town)
fetch	get

Chapter 4 Appendix *Continued*

Lexical Differences: Appalachian Dialect	
Dialect Word	Standard English Equivalent
tote	carry
cher	chair
risins	boils
pert'n near	almost
sack	paper bag
look at him	talk to him
stoved up	injured
pocket book	purse
plum	very
reckon	believe
holler	shout
right smart	a considerable amount

*This section lists some of the syntactic differences between standard and black dialectal English. From J. Baratz, "Teaching Reading in an Urban Negro School System," in J.C. Baratz and R.W. Shuy (eds.), *Teaching Black Children to Read* (Arlington, VA: Center for Applied Linguistics, 1969), pp. 99–100. Copyright 1969 by the Center for Applied Linguistics. Reprinted by permission.

†These expressions in particular are being used by establishment speakers with increasing frequency.

5

The Law and
Educational
Programming

Public Policy and Legal Precedents

Individuals outside the middle-class mainstream continue to be denied true educational opportunity owing to the still prevalent and institutionalized prejudices of our teaching and helping philosophies. The fate of the culturally linguistically nonstandard and limited-English-proficient (LEP) speakers of English is a case in point. These speakers generally perform poorly in school; their achievement scores, particularly in reading, are uniformly low.

Congressional commitment to improving educational opportunity for the underclass and working poor of our society has been limited to a plethora of programs that entail eradicationist or noninterventionist teaching philosophies. For example, in both traditional Head Start and Chapter One programs, the nonstandard and rule-governed dialectal utterances of the culturally different children are frequently eliminated or ignored. In most cases the attainment of acceptable standard-English-speaking skills are not achieved by these children. And without such aural–oral skills, educational literacy (visuo-graphic abilities) is difficult to achieve. Logic dictates that a significant interrelationship exists among hearing and understanding, talking, reading, and writing skills.

Supreme Court Decision

The Supreme Court's commitment to educational equality for all, regardless of cultural membership, is exemplified in the landmark *Brown v. the Topeka Board of*

Education decision (1954), which stated the following:

> *In these days it is doubtful that any child may reasonably be expected to succeed in life if he is denied the opportunity of an education. Such an opportunity, where the state has undertaken to provide it, is a right which must be made available to all* on equal terms. *[p. 493; emphasis added]*

This decision impacts upon all children regardless of their race, ethnicity, or social class membership. Furthermore, the words "on equal terms" would suggest that all American children should have an equal educational opportunity to learn.

Lower Court Decisions Relevant to Equal Educational Activities

Lower courts have mandated a number of decisions relevant to appropriate testing and placement, as well as classroom activity for culturally different and poor students. For example, the *Hobsen v. Hansen* (1969) lawsuit questioned the appropriateness of an academic tracking system for students that was based on biased standardized test scores. This decision was immediately followed by *Diana v. the California State Board of Education* (1970), which also addressed the issue of student placement based on standardized tests utilizing test information and directions in standard English and their resultant biased scores when the testees were primarily Spanish-speaking students. In 1975, *Lora v. the New York Board of Education* was first brought to the attention of the United States District Court in New York and was considered over the next nine years; its adjudication in 1984 mentions due process rights related to linguistic, cultural, or ethnic background differences. Starting in 1979, a variety of court cases involved litigation along similar lines as *Lora*: for example, *PASE v. Hannon* (1980) and *Marshall v. McDaniel* (1984) were concerned with discriminatory intent, whereas *Mattie T. v. Holladay* (1979), *Larry P. v. Riles* (1979), and *Alexander v. Choate* (1985) were concerned with discriminatory effects of assessment/placement procedures.

Lau v. Nichols (1974) was among the first major pieces of litigation that dealt with nonnative speakers of English. This was followed by the *Bilingual Education Act* of 1974, which calls for bilingual programming for LEP students. Although this act was concerned with students coming from linguistically different environments, its provisions did not extend to the nonstandard English speaker.

The Landmark King Case and Language Barriers to Learning

The problem of the nonstandard English speaker was addressed in the *Martin Luther King Junior Elementary School Children v. the Ann Arbor School District Board* (1979). Judge Charles Joiner ruled that a language difference—African–American

English—did indeed exist. However, the judge did not believe that the difference in itself constituted a barrier to learning but rather that the children's learning was impeded by the teachers' unconscious negative attitudes to African–American English. To obviate these attitudes, Judge Joiner mandated that specific measures be taken to educate the teachers regarding the dialectal conflict. Basically, the plan is built around the idea of a 20-hour teacher in-service program. (See page 26 for the topics presented in the program.)

Although the effects of the judicial act have not attenuated the educational problems of the students at King School, it has accomplished the following: (1) the recognition of African–American English (and by implication, other social class dialects) as a legitimate dialect; (2) the importance of attitudinal influences in education (e.g., the Pygmalion or Rosenthal effects); (3) the inadequacy of teacher in-service training vis-à-vis nonstandard speakers; and (4) the suggestion that existing educational programs for nonstandard speakers are similarly ineffective.

Some Interesting Details of the King Case

1. The Green Road Project (GRP) is located in an affluent white area in Ann Arbor and mainly houses low-income blacks. The children from the GRP attend the Martin Luther King Jr. Elementary School and comprise 13 percent of the school population. Eighty percent of the students are white and the remaining 7 percent are Asian and Latin.

2. The black children were performing poorly in the school; many of them were labeled as learning disordered, behavior problems, and the like. But the mothers believed their children were normal and instituted a lawsuit.

3. On July 28, 1977, the case was brought to the Federal Court of Judge Charles Joiner.

4. At the outset Judge Joiner rejected the allegations of the plaintiffs—that the GRP children were culturally, socially, and economically deprived, and that they had been labeled "learning disabled" and "emotionally impaired" without due consideration of their cultural and racial background. He also dismissed the allegation that the case feel under the "equal protection" clause of the Constitution. He said, "No law or clause of the Constitution of the United States explicitly secures the rights of plaintiffs to special educational services to overcome unsatisfactory academic performance based on cultural, social, or economic background" (Labov 1982, p. 169).

5. But the judge did retain one of the plaintiffs' notions, that the defendant school board had failed to take appropriate action to overcome language barriers, in violation of Title 20 of the U.S. Code, Section 1703 (f):

No state shall deny equal educational opportunity to an individual on account of his or her race, color, sex, or national origin by . . . (f) the failure by an

> *educational agency to take appropriate action to overcome linguistic barriers*
> *that impede equal participation by its students in its instructional program.*

Judge Joiner also quoted President Nixon who in a 1972 message to Congress said, "School authorities must take appropriate action to overcome *whatever* (Judge's emphasis) language barriers exist . . . . This would establish, in effect, an educational bill of rights for Mexican–Americans, Puerto Ricans, Indians, and *others who start under language handicaps*" (Labov 1982, p. 169; italics added).

6.   Thus, the judge concluded that the allegations in the King case, involving inferior education as related to cultural, social, or socioeconomic barriers, were not legally tenable, but that those that were related to language barriers were of significance, and that the plaintiffs had to show that the defendant school board had neglected to overcome the language barriers.

7.   It is important to understand that when the case was first filed, it was approached by the plaintiffs' lawyers in terms of legal, political, and economic issues. But the judge's ruling made the peripheral issue of language differences into the central issue confronting the court.

A Critique of the King Case

1.   An important interrelationship exists between oral standard English acquisition and literacy. Standard-English-speaking skills can best be obtained through a system of mandatory teaching of bidialectalism and biculturalism..

2..   Bidialectalism and biculturalism, as well as the attitudinal changes, may have to be legally effectuated.

3.   Since the King case demonstrated minimum gains achieved by the children insofar as their reading skills are concerned, it would appear (a) that teacher attitudinal effects, by themselves, are not as important as suggested, and/or (b) that conventional in-service training is ineffective in altering any of the teachers' preconceived biases, or (c) that language differences or interference is of significant importance insofar as reading failure is concerned, or (d) that a combination of negative stereotypical biases and language problems impact profoundly upon reading–educational skill acquisition.

4.   Co-jointly with the implementation of such a program, there should also be an in-depth and intensive in-service program for teachers designed to alter any negative attitudinal preconceptions they may hold regarding these children (see Appendix B).

Summary Statements

1.   If the sociopolitical climate in our country is such that the removal of dialectal and attitudinal barriers to effective education for poor children is untenable, then the possibility of state or federal legal recourse to their removal may be appropriate (see Appendixes C and D). Historically, there is a precedent for such a recommendation. Clearly Congress, as well as our state legislatures and courts, have been concerned with related issues. Judge Joiner, in his landmark 1979 Ann Arbor decision, gave valid reason for such a recommendation.

2.   Furthermore, in 1982, a report commissioned by the National Academy of Sciences (Heller, Holtzman, and Messick 1982) suggested that rather than focus on the issue of bias in testing, as so many of our court decisions have done, we should address the issue of what kinds of effective services can be provided to these children.

3.   Both dialectal and attitudinal barriers must be addressed; either one by itself would probably prove to be unsatisfactory.

4.   A bidialectal–bicultural teaching philosophy should be adopted in kindergarten for nonstandard-English-speaking children.

6

Nonstandard
Language:
Its Assessment

Assessment of Nonstandard Speakers:
Some General Comments*

The significance of a test score in our society is patently important. For example, it may signify potential success or lack of it; it may tell us whether the test taker is functioning at an appropriate performance level; it may provide us with relevant diagnostic information that is germane to a successful program or inappropriate and biased information that triggers a negative reaction.

For these and other reasons, test scores may have a profound impact upon the testee, and it is of obvious importance that these scores be both valid and reliable; that is, that they reveal what they are supposed to reveal and that they are replicable. Frequently, language test scores, as well as other kinds of tests, are neither valid nor replicable.

What is language? It is both linguistic and paralinguistic codes by which we express our ideas and feelings, by which we communicate our thoughts. Thus, items used on tests should focus on the language codes used by speakers and listeners of the same linguistic community; this is a culturally fair and valid definition of language.

---

*As noted in the title, this chapter stresses the testing of nonstandard speakers; Chapter 7 discusses the testing of nonnative speakers of English. However, both chapters contain information germane to the nonstandard and the nonnative speakers of English.

Appropriate Procedures

Further, the assessment tool should involve appropriate procedures for analyzing the results of the test. Thus, if a language sample is desired in order to evaluate the speaker's use of his or her language system, one must arrange for this sample to be obtained in different speaker–listener interactions. Pragmatic analyses have shown that such interactions, and their subsequent language samples, vary as a function of whom the child is talking to, where he is doing the talking, and so on. To do otherwise would not elicit a valid communication sample that could be generalized to different communicative situations. For example, a supervisor once noted that a culturally different and poor child who was noted as being an essentially nonverbal person based upon his fragmentary language samples was indeed a very verbal child when speaking on his own "turf" and to his own peers.

Culturally Biased Scores and Validity

Whether a test score is valid is also dependent upon the interpretation of the test score. Thus, on the one hand, if one wants to find out how effective a nonstandard-speaking child's communicative skills are in the classroom, a low score on a test standardized on standard-English-speaking children (therefore a culturally biased test) might show that the child does not possess sufficient verbal skills for adequate interaction in the classroom. Such an interpretation would be valid and present important information to the teacher.

On the other hand, if one interprets the results as suggesting the child has inferior or retarded language skills per se, this would be an invalid interpretation. Therefore, a culturally biased test, one that has been normed on a given sample of people from a particular social class or culture or geographic residence, may be a valid or invalid test depending upon how the results are interpreted.

For example, are Civil Service Tests, College Entrance Exams, academic grades—or any tests dependent upon a knowledge of the standard English linguistic code—biased and thus invalid? Not so, if the results are interpreted to disclose whether the testee can function adequately in an environment in which the mainstream and establishment dialect (and culture) is desired. They are only invalid if they are said to show that such test takers possess inferior skills or knowledge per se.

Summary

Culturally biased tests may contain a deliberate or nondeliberate bias:

1. A deliberate bias is characterized by the insertion of test items not representative of the speaker's dialect community or culture but designed to elicit information about the testee's understanding or use of the mainstream dialect or culture.

2. A nondeliberate and nondesirable bias may reflect a test normed or standardized on mainstream society, administered to a nonmember of this society, and interpreted to suggest he or she possesses inferior skills.

Culture-fair tests evaluate the children's *use* of their language within *their* dialect community (see Appendix L for samples of dialect interference on some selected tests). Thus, we must be sensitive to the sample population on which the test was standardized, the items used on the test, and the way the test is interpreted.

Test Reliability

The ability to replicate the test score undergirds test reliability. If a test score is not repeatable, it is not only unreliable, it is potentially dangerous. We cannot build appropriate educational or habilitative strategies and plans upon inadequate and/or incorrect test results.

There are three major sources of error in the implementation of reliable tests: the tester, the situation, and the topic.

1. *Tester.* Assessment specialists may vary as a function of their sex, age, race, and status. Thus a tester with different characteristics may seem "strange" to some children. This unfamiliarity may precipitate a negative feeling from the testee and might affect his or her responses to the test. It is therefore important that some time be spent in free play previous to the testing; in this way, the anxiety engendered by unfamiliarity may be attenuated and therefore more reliable test measures obtained.

2. *Test situation or setting.* Assessment may take place in a clinic, school, home, playground, or other physical location. Clearly, a strange or unfamiliar environment can create undesirable amounts of anxiety that can negatively affect test scores. Thus, as just noted, time must be spent prior to the testing to acquaint the child with the environment. If you believe that a child's test score may vary significantly as a function of where the testing occurs (e.g., the clinic or the home) then this bias must be eliminated.

3. *Topic.* If the topic is of little or no significance to one child, or conversely, of much interest to another child, it can obviously have an impact upon a given child's response pattern. Thus, if a pragmatic language sample is to be obtained (how the child uses language in different social contexts), then the topic used should be culture fair.

Reporting the Results

Reporting the results of an evaluation can patently affect a child's classroom placement and teaching–treating strategies that are to be employed, as indicated by the following examples.

1. *Interpreting an invalid (culturally biased) test—a test that was normed or standardized on a sample population not relevant to the child:* Compare the child's test score to the standardized norms (this will tell the reader how the child performs relevant to standard English speakers—the language code of the classroom). However, the test score should also be compared to the child's peer group in order to obtain a true reflection of his or her language skills. (If peer group norms are not available, perform an item analysis on the test data—that is, point out items you know or believe are culturally biased. See Appendix L.)

2. The way these test data are reported can obviously affect the teaching–treating strategy to be employed.

3. *Classroom placement as a function of the diagnostic label "Mentally Retarded" versus "Functionally (or Educationally) Retarded":* Most states now require that a child possess an IQ score of less than 70 plus failure on an adaptive behavior test before he or she is labeled as being mentally retarded (MR). Therefore, a child with a passing grade regarding adaptive behavior but with a relatively low IQ score is to be considered as being functionally or educationally retarded, not MR.

Placement of such a child into a resource room would appear to be contraindicated. This child possesses the intellectual potential to learn school skills, but for some reason (in part, we suspect dialectal and cultural conflicts relevant to the unicultural teaching strategy employed) the child has not acquired the literate skills expected of children his or her age.

Placement of such a child into a bidialectal–bicultural program in which the teacher's attitude has been carefully evaluated and transformed, if necessary, would be more appropriate. Certainly, labeling such a child as mentally retarded, which is quite common, and placing the child in a special classroom for the mentally retarded is contraindicated.

The format of the report must address, therefore, the educational implications of the test data. If not, incorrect and/or inappropriate placement will occur.

4. *How the reporting of test scores can misinterpret the truth:* Careful examination of the test data is important if a valid interpretation is to be obtained. For example, when the Scholastic Aptitude Test (SAT) scores were reported in 1981 by race and ethnic groups, it was noted that students from low-income families scored lower than students from high-income families; African–American students scored on an average 110 points lower than the white students. But additional analyses revealed that most of the African–American students who were tested came from low-income (i.e., lower-class) families, and it was these students, therefore, who scored low; the higher income black students scored as high as did their white counterparts. These latter data, however, were not reported and the reader was left with the impression that African–Americans as a race are inferior to the Caucasian race.

There is a growing tide of concern regarding the significant numbers of children being misclassified or overclassified as "handicapped" based upon the former type of reporting and being placed in resource rooms. This process occurs because the standardized testing used is a convenient and expedient means of classifying children and thus excluding children from regular classrooms. It also fosters the creation of a dual education system. Additionally, the process is of little or no use in formulating instructional programs for students classified as educationally or functionally retarded.

Testing Alternatives

If standardized tests are inappropriate for use—that is, if they do not reveal the normative data required relative to the child's cultural peer group—what alternatives are available to the tester? In an article by Fay Boyd Vaughn-Cooke (1983), seven different alternatives to traditional tests are presented and discussed. These alternatives are as follows:

1. Standardize existing tests on nonmainstream English speakers.
2. Include a small percentage of minorities in the standardization sample when developing a test.
3. Modify or revise existing tests in ways that will make them appropriate for nonmainstream speakers.
4. Utilize a language sample when assessing the language of nonmainstream speakers.
5. Utilize criterion-referenced measures when assessing the language of nonmainstream speakers.
6. Refrain from using all standardized tests that have not been corrected for test bias when assessing the language of nonmainstream speakers.
7. Develop a new test that can provide a more appropriate assessment of the language of nonmainstream English speakers.

Summary Statement

It is suggested that the following tests and test interpretation be performed by the clinician.

1. As is reported in some detail in Chapter 8, a language sample utilizing at least two different examiners (e.g., clinician and mother) in two different situations (e.g. clinic/school and home) be obtained. The protocol shown on pages 127–133 can be used to obtain information regarding the child's pragmatic use of language, the severity of his or her dialect, and the presence of any communicative disorders.

2. Culturally biased standardized tests, frequently required by public school systems, can be used if item analyses are performed. Thus, if the test was normed on a population sample not relevant to the testee, the child's so-called incorrect response(s) should be analyzed to determine if they are deficient or linguistically

different. These determinations can be made by virtue of (a) your knowledge of the dialect and (b) reference to material relevant to the dialect (see pertinent appendixes for such information). Such a determination can inform the clinician and teacher which utterances need to be eradicated because they are, in fact, incorrect for both the mainstream (classroom) community and for the child's peer linguistic community. This child requires treatment for his or her linguistic deficiencies. Those utterances valid in the latter community but nonstandard in the classroom need to be taught through code-switching techniques—that is, "school language" versus "everyday language"—a bidialectal approach.

Scoring the test by eliminating the nonstandard patterns from consideration (since they are not errors but rule-governed differences) will obviously increase the score obtained by the child and allow for a more valid understanding of the child's linguistic competence.

Variables Affecting Test Scores

Situational

The culturally different child is influenced not only by what he has learned, but also by what surrounds him at any particular time. It is particularly important for the speech–language clinician to remember that when a child—any child—uses language, it is used in a situation and for a purpose; its use has some point. To understand language in its social context requires understanding the meanings that social contexts and uses of language have for their participants. Language must be studied in its social contexts, in terms of its organization to serve social ends.

Language is both determined by and determinative of the reactions of the users to the physical, cultural, and social environmental conditions and situations in which language plays a part. Thus, the speech–language specialist (SLS) must realize that subcultural differences in language use, such as fluency or syntactic complexity, may appear more or less pronounced depending on one or more factors of the speech situation in which the language samples are obtained. The speaker characteristics present in one situation may often represent an interaction with task, topic, or elicitation condition rather than fixed or universal characteristics of the speakers.

If an SLS is to appreciate the importance of situational variables to the evaluations of and interactions with culturally different children, then it is essential to be aware of what constitutes a situational variable. Many authors have devised several different categories of situational variables; however, the basic concepts remain the same. There are eight components of speech: (1) setting a scene, (2) participants or personnel, (3) ends (goals and outcomes), (4) art characteristics (message form and topic), (5) key (tone, manner, or spirit in which an act is done), (6) instrumentalities (the channel—oral, written, etc.—and code—language or dialect), (7) norms of interactions and interpretation, and (8) genres (types of speech—conversation, cursing, lecture, sales pitch, etc.). There are also five categories of situational differences: (1) topic, (2) task, (3) listener(s), (4) interactions, and (5) situations with mixed characteristics. Figure 6-1 has compressed these situational variables into four factors:

Test variables

Physical situation variables

Tester/testee variables

Communication variables

As can be seen, although the number and names of various categories differ, the basic concept remains constant in the categorization systems cited above.

All of the components of the situational variables appear to be quite logical. Their validity can hardly be questioned, and it is easy to see that the various contexts must necessarily play a very important role in language usage. Surprisingly, the tendency in child-language research has been to ignore situational variables or to combine speech data from several contexts. Another grave defect in many studies has been the failure to state precisely (1) the difference and (2) the interrelationship between values pertaining to the sociolinguistic feature, on the one hand, and the values pertaining to the social context in which it can occur, on the other.

Personal Contexts

It is obvious that the people involved in a situation shape that situation and affect the communication. When a child who is normally quite verbal and active comes into the presence of a stranger (especially an adult stranger), he, unless he is extremely outgoing, will immediately become quite silent and shy. Imagine this same child being thrust into a situation with an adult who, from physical appearances (color of

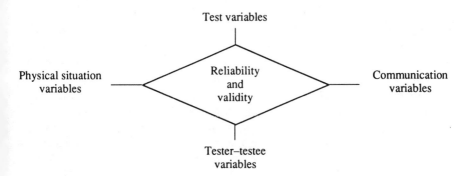

FIGURE 6-1   Variables Affecting Test Reliability and Validity

the skin, clothing, etc.), looks quite unlike any of the adults with whom the child has come into contact in his environment. And, to compound the problem, when the adult begins to speak, she is using different words and in some ways a different language from the child, for example, "Come and sit down," "Look at my pictures," "Tell me what you see."

Obviously, this situation would be somewhat traumatic for almost any child. Yet, in classrooms and therapy settings teachers and speech clinicians are exposing culturally different children to this type of situation.

Teachers and SLSs appear no less frightening to a culturally different child than, for example, does a dentist to most children. Although the SLS cannot change his or her own personal background, there are several ways in which the effects of personal context upon evaluations of and interactions with culturally different children can be obviated. First, when analyzing what a child says, it is important for the SLS to ask him or herself to whom the child was speaking. Conversely, when looking at how a child responds to someone else's speech, it is wise to ask who the speaker was—for that may be as much the cause of the child's response as what was said. Second, in attempting to elicit speech samples from a culturally different child, it is wise to remember that conversation is more likely to occur when it is initiated by the child rather than by the adult. Also, it has been found that adult commands to initiate action more frequently provoke verbal reply than do commands to desist an action. Finally, the SLS must be aware of the Pygmalion (Rosenthal) effect—that is, the attitudes that language may elicit in the listener. Certain language forms may lead to the SLS's stereotyping of children from particular ethnic groups. This stereotyping plays a key role in the process of speech rating. Rather than solely evaluating the "correctness" of a child's language and speech, the SLS should weigh heavily the appropriateness of the child's speech with regard to the particular speech situation.

Message Context

What has been said previously in a conversation can have a very definite effect upon the current conversation. For example, if someone says to you "You are a dummy," your reaction to the statement will depend upon what preceded the statement. If at the time you were sitting in a math class and happened to answer a homework problem incorrectly, your reaction to the statement would most probably be one of hurt embarrassment. If, on the other hand, the statement had followed a silly joke you had just told, your reaction would likely be one of good humor and friendship.

Similarly, what an SLS says to a culturally different child will have a very definite effect upon his or her emotional, behavioral, and speech responses. In giving directions or in general conversation, the SLS must analyze not only what to say, but also the way in which to say it. How does it sound to the child? Does he really understand what has been said, or is he inferring something entirely different from the intent?

A wise SLS will remember that a child will respond in the manner in which he believes he is expected to respond. When a child is asked to perform, a part of his rationale for his particular behavior will be determined by whether he expects to be praised for his efforts or whether he expects to be punished for his errors.

Naturally, there are no specific rules that govern what an SLS can say to a child or the way in which it can be said. Therefore, in order to ascertain whether a child perceives what is said as it was intended, the SLS must observe the child's reactions. If he did not react as might have been expected, this may indicate the necessity for rephrasing the previous statement. Through this method of observation—readjustment—the clinician becomes more adept at "catering" to the needs of the particular child.

The SLS must also remember that a child must be rewarded for his or her efforts and not necessarily for the correctness of his or her responses. Punishment for errors rarely leads to correction of these errors; more often than not, punishment results in a discontinuation of responses altogether. Therefore, the way in which an SLS reacts to a child's performance will have a great effect upon the child's succeeding responses.

Content Context

Topic, per se, is a regulator of language use. Anyone who knows children realizes that the topic being discussed influences their participation in the conversation. All people of all ages prefer to talk about things they are interested in, and children talk more about subjects with which they are personally involved. Moreover, the greater the degree of affect or personal involvement in the topic of conversation, the greater the likelihood of structural complexity.

Unfortunately, educational practices often fail to take into account what topics motivate students. Teaching methods designed without appreciation of this situational dimension often fall upon deaf student ears.

In selecting materials for speech therapy, the SLS must be aware of the effect of the topics presented by the materials on the responses of the children. Pictures depicting "Dick, Jane, and Sally" at work and at play may be quite suitable for the middle-class child, but they will be of little interest to the culturally different child. this is not to say that the SLS should feel limited in presenting materials that deal only with the immediate environment of the child. Novel, surprising, and incongruous items frequently elicit enthusiastic responses from culturally different children. Therefore, it is incumbent upon the SLS to select materials and topics for conversation that are necessarily of interest to the children. And there may be no better way to find appropriate material than to present assorted varieties of materials utilizing various methods of presentation and to observe the amount of interest each generates.

Task Content

When a person, child or adult, speaks, he or she usually has a purpose or reason for speaking. Therefore, in looking at an utterance, it is useful to pose the question, What is the speaker trying to do?

Communication differences between different social classes may be primarily in the area of how language is used rather than in the sphere of linguistic development. For example, if the question "How are you today?" were asked, a middle-class speaker might respond, "Just fine, thanks," whereas an African–American speaker might respond, "I be right fine." There can be no question that both speakers intended to convey the message that they are in good health, and both successfully did so. The response of the latter speaker would not be considered to be grammatically correct according to the rules of standard English. Yet an analysis of the response of the middle-class speaker reveals that, although it would be perfectly acceptable to all speakers of standard English, it is not syntactically correct—it is not a complete sentence!

Teachers and SLSs alike are guilty of placing what is perhaps too much emphasis on the way in which something is said rather than on *what* is actually being said. The basic reason we use language is to convey an idea. Therefore, it is well to remember that a speaker who loses the idea he is trying to convey because of elaborate, though correct, lexicon and grammar is a *less* effective speaker than one who can convey his meaning regardless of linguistic form. We must be careful to examine children's speech in terms of task context, and we will often be less concerned with details of grammar and more concerned with appropriateness of content.

Another aspect of task context deals with the goal that the teacher and/or SLS sets for the child—that is, what they are asking the child to do and the way in which they are asking him or her to do it. It is obvious that the particular task that the child is asked to perform will affect the manner in which he or she performs it. A child's familiarity with a task (how often he or she is exposed to similar tasks in the home environment) will determine how well and how easily he or she performs. Therefore, in evaluating a child's performance on a particular task it is important to consider the child's familiarity with that task.

Surrounding Physical Context

The physical context in which communication takes place is of great importance. Children are even more sensitive to physical context than are adults, and they use it more in their communication. They are, of course, apprehensive about new environments.

The social situation is comprised of a relationship between the place (locale) and time. Thus, if a particular child is in a familiar situation and happens to feel well (and feels like talking) at that particular time, then a speech sample obtained under these circumstances would probably contain more verbalizations with greater structural complexities than would a sample obtained from the same child under negative conditions of place and time.

Thus, a child sitting in a therapy room will be influenced by the immediate surroundings in the room, by how he or she personally feels at that particular time, and by background (or past) experiences. At any one time one of these three situations is likely to be influencing the child more than the others. The SLS must determine which of the variables is affecting the child and whether this effect is positive or negative. If the situational effects are felt to be negative, the SLS should carefully guard the observations made during that particular session, for they are not likely to be truly representative of that child.

7

Management of
Nonstandard Speakers

Previous Research Programs

Education in early childhood from its beginning has been primarily concerned with enriching and supporting the optimum growth of children. Nursery schools, which were developed as an extension of home life to help enrich children's total development, stated psychological and physical nurture as objectives. With the advent of the "critical periods" hypothesis in the early 1960s, more and more attention was given to the field of early education as infant and toddler programs were born. For the optimum development of a child, it was assumed that physical and psychological environments must be enriched as early in life as possible because environmental effects are greatest in the early and more rapid periods of intellectual development. When the "critical periods" theory was beginning to take hold, history once again turned to a humanitarian impulse such as the one of the 1880s and 1890s that spurred the birth of the kindergarten. In the early 1960s similar social urgencies brought compensatory education on the scene.

With America's changing lifestyles, more concern is being given to compensatory early childhood education in general, and to children of low-income families in particular. Statistics concerning the changing lifestyles report millions of children are now being reared by single parents. The majority of all American mothers with school-age children are working outside the home, two-thirds of them in full-time jobs. It is quite evident that the curricula of preschool educational programs are of increasing importance to these mothers and to others who make use of these programs.

Compensatory Curricula

One of the most important questions to be asked of any educational intervention program or treatment strategy is whether the learner has sufficiently acquired the skills or educational content being transmitted to her. A justification of the continuance of any program is obviously in its success. Since the poor and culturally different child has apparently not demonstrated significant improvement in acquisition of skills or content—that is, the quality of her educational input still remains at a low level relative to her middle-class peer—it can only be assumed that program effectiveness has been minimal.

The various programs designed to enhance learning abilities and performance levels are based generally upon the malnutrition model, which holds to the point of view that the child must be force-fed those cognitive nutrients commensurate to those utilized by the "establishment." A variety of educational and clinical strategies have been employed relevant to this model, the thesis being that development of readiness or cognitive skills in poor children was distorted or impaired and that subsequent language learning and the acquisition of academic or content-type subjects were bound to be negatively affected.

Compensatory Programs—An Overview

Head Start initiated compensatory programming for poor five- to six-year-old children in 1965; it was complemented by intervention programs that initiated training at younger age levels—3 or 4 years of age. At present infant education or stimulation programs have become the vogue. A variety of parent education programs have also been developed to supplement the various child and infant education programs. Thus it was decided that "compensatory" programs be developed for disadvantaged children before they entered the compulsory school programs. The objective of such programs was to "enrich" these children so that their "readiness" level would more equate, or more nearly so, that of the "establishment" child, for whom our educational system is geared.

In the late sixties and seventies, protagonists of early environmental intervention suggested that the various programs show fair levels of success—that they have not failed. But others did not support this premise and indicate that the intervention allowed for some demonstrable gains during preschool but does not carry over into elementary school.

Head Start programs were developed to provide an early education for the preschool child. It was hoped that with these opportunities, the educational problems of the poor child in elementary school would be, if not eliminated, at least significantly attenuated.

The results, however, do not appear to generally support this ideal. Although there are numerous exceptions, the fact remains that Head Start educated children seem to be experiencing the same rate of academic failure and disillusionment as do other poor children. The reason certainly does not lie with the skills or the enthusiasm of the Head Start staff but rather, as pointed out in the following pages, the failure of the compensatory philosophy they adhere to. It should also be noted that Head Start provides many other services to poor children and their families other than educational intervention. For example, the health and nutrition services and the parent education and counseling provided are of inestimable value to the participants in these programs.

Head Start initiated the first major effort to provide preschool programming for poor children. The program's expressed purpose was to provide education to children from low-income families in an effort to compensate for these children's inadequate experimental background and thus bring them up to the level of middle-class children by the time they entered school. A rather wide variety of philosophies and models characterized the different programs. Some were quite similar to the traditional nursery school in that they provided a permissive and minimally structured learning situation; they provided a great deal of general enrichment such as field trips and verbal stimulation. Others provided highly structured learning environments by formally teaching cognitive and verbal skills.

Almost all Head Start and the better day care centers and nursery programs provide a number of skills, the most important of which is the development of language skills. Since the preschool years are the most important for language development and allow for the rapid growth of oral language skills, it is obviously a developmental stage of much concern to preschool specialists. A number of different formalized learning as well as incidental learning techniques have been used to enhance the language skills of the children. For example, a process of heavy verbal bombardment with the teacher maintaining a steady stream of questions and comments has been used in some programs. Others have used games that encourage oral language usage, such as play-talking on the phone. Some programs systematically taught language skills to children using behavior modification techniques.

Another major goal of such programs is the teaching of percepts and concepts, particularly those categories or classes of things that are learned through visual processing activities. Examples are the teaching of color, size, and shape recognition; discrimination; and sequencing. Less importance is usually attached to auditory processing. If what is heard and understood—the auditory function of language—is basic to academic skill acquisition, then teaching programs must stress auditory as well as visual processing strategies.

Among other skills taught to children in preschool programs are gross and fine motor skills, social skills, and self-help skills, as well as the attainment of a positive self-image and an expectancy of success.

An analysis of the effectiveness of Head Start programming reveals that, in general, children score higher on post-tests than when starting the program. In comparison to middle-class children, they generally hold their own in the first and second grades, but they often fall behind their middle-class peers in the third, fourth, or fifth grades.

Infant education programs came into being in response to the apparent failure of the other intervention-type programs. It was noted that one of the reasons for this lack of relative success was due to the child's established cognitive and linguistic behavior. It was suggested that, for intervention to be successful, it would have to be initiated before the child established these behavioral patterns—hence, the need for infant education.

The Fallacy of the Compensatory Program

The essential fallacy of the compensatory program lies in the assumption that personal deficiencies account for the educational failures of the child. But when failure reaches such massive proportions, as it has in these programs, it is necessary to look at other possible causes; for example, the social and cultural obstacles to learning and the inability of the school to adjust to the social situation. Operation Head Start is designed to repair the child rather than the school. To the extent that it is based upon this inverted logic, it is bound to fail.

A second area in which the compensatory approach is doing serious harm to our educational system concerns the consequences of failure and the reaction to it. The fault is found not in the data, the theory, or the methods used, but rather in the children who have failed to respond to opportunities offered them. When poor children fail to show the significant advance that the deprivation theory predicts, it is further proof, for those who support the contention, of the gulf that separates their mental processes form those of "the biologically superior middle class."

When intervention or enrichment programs such as Head Start failed in their stated purpose, programs were designed to initiate the training of these children very early in their lives through parent involvement in infant education.

Failure as Related to the American School System

The American school system, whether public or private, is predominantly a middle-class institution. It not only teaches middle-class values and ideals, but it operates in a middle-class fashion and uses middle-class methods in performing its role in American society. This is inevitable since the official ideology of the United States is a middle-class ideology, and the school system is an institutionalized arm of that middle-class society. The educators who staff the school system are themselves largely middle class or have adopted middle-class values—since they are products of the system, that is to be expected. Because they are based on middle-class values and ideals, the public school system and its methods have not made headway in educating the economically disadvantaged. Although there has been scattered piecemeal success, the school system as a whole has failed in this effort.

Failure as Related to Compensatory Education for the Disadvantaged

Current educational programs for the economically disadvantaged are based on the assumption that the individual from a poor and/or different culture is actually culturally deprived. Therefore, attempts to alter the plight of the child have involved "enriching" his environment or administering him a "dose of culture." The most widely endorsed strategy for helping disadvantaged children is one called "enrichment." In broad terms, enrichment attempts to compress into an educational program the maximum quantity of experience believed to contribute to the culturally privileged child's superiority in learning. Those educators who advocate this type of compensatory education claim that the poverty child lags behind his middle-class counterpart in preparation for school and that he or she is experientially, linguistically, and socially retarded—that is, he or she is culturally deficient or deprived. Thus, preschool intervention has been advocated by "deficit" theorists as a means for lessening the gap between the disadvantaged child's capabilities at school age and the requirements of a middle-class educational system. In order for the culturally deprived child to overcome his deficits (deficiencies), he must adopt the behavior, especially the language behavior, of mainstream society.

Most teachers have certain evaluational reactions to their students' speech that are stereotyped versions of their attitudes toward the speaker. A child's speech may thus serve as an index and identification of his culture, and when the teacher encounters such a culturally different child, he or she perhaps subconsciously expects nonstandardness, reticence, and uncertainty from the child. Interestingly, the child may also have developed a particular stereotyped and negative attitude toward the teacher.

Teacher–pupil expectations affect teacher–pupil interactions. A child who is treated as though she were reticent, insecure, and a representative of that which is substandard will react as such. She will feel that, because of her inferior language behavior, she herself, and all that she represents, is inferior. Because she has to acquire her education in an unfamiliar and unnatural language, she will suffer frustration and educational alienation. Her entire life-style, which is also that of her parents and those with whom she associates, has been rejected by that institution which purportedly exists to supply her with the tools to succeed in American society.

Perhaps the most important factor in determining educational success is whether the child feels he has some control over his life. If the unique heritage from which he comes is destroyed by efforts to make him acceptable to an ideal social norm, the resultant human being can only feel powerless in a majority society.

Compensatory education, then, is an educational failure for most children, for it is destroying them psychologically and educationally by trying to prepare them for mainstream society. Concomitantly, it alienates them from the culture and language of their peer communities.*

A Sample Preschool Program: A Two-Phase Approach

In view of the apparent failure of compensatory programming to adequately prepare the child for a successful school career, and because aural–oral language is the touchstone on which successful academic achievement must rest, we initiated a noncompensatory program for preschool children in the early 1970s. Bidialectal programs were not new—an experimental program had been developed for African–American school-age children in the Chicago public schools—and some programs had been developed for bilingual children (mainly Spanish-speaking children). Our program addressed the needs of preschool, mainly white, children attending three experimental and three control Head Start classrooms in Knox County, Tennessee.

The primary group used in this research on bidialectalism consisted predominantly of four- and five-year-old children. Most of the procedures presented in this section were developed and refined in an experimental pilot study performed in the Pediatric Language Laboratory (PLL)), a preschool program sponsored by the Department of Audiology and Speech Pathology of the University of Tennessee. The program was conducted for approximately seven months, from November through May.

The study team felt that before the actual teaching program began, it was essential to determine exactly what specific items of dialect are encountered in the black and white population in this Appalachian area. The work of other authors in cities in the North and in West Virginia was used a reference guide for the collection of the speech samples. These samples were collected for a period of approximately two months in both groups. Several methods were used:

1. Spontaneous transcriptions recorded by teachers, clinicians, and the authors while the child was in the classroom, in therapy sessions, or in small play groups (this was the primary method used in the Head Start program)

---

*Many states are now adopting compulsory competency testing and the attainment of specified scores for eighth grade as well as potential high school graduates. That is, before these children will be allowed to graduate they will have to demonstrate proficiency or, at least competency, in basic academic skills. We support such testing; we believe all high school graduates should be able to read and write with some basic skills. It is our conviction, however, that the larger majority of children who will fail the test and not be allowed to graduate until such time as the test is passed will be the lower-class or poor children. When such children fail these tests one, or possibly two or more times, dependent upon state laws, questions will inevitably be raised relevant to the genetic inferiority of these children and absolute statements made—"They are simply too dumb to learn." We submit, as suggested in the text, it is the professional worker and the teaching strategy employed that may be at fault, not the child.

2. Analysis of certain tests such as the Peabody Picture Vocabulary Test to ascertain items differing from standard English
3. Remote telemetry recordings that allowed taping of children in therapy or at play

The latter was used mainly with the PLL group. An effort was made to take samples from each child in both the school environment and the playground situation.

Once the samples were taken, they were analyzed by noting the similarities and differences of grammatical structures, lexical items, and phonological output among the different transcriptions of the children's speech as related to standard English. Standard English was operationally defined as the socially prestigious language patterns accepted and used by middle-class speakers (particularly, school teachers) in this area. Members of the child's cultural community were then questioned to ascertain if the dialectal features were still prominent in the area. "Dialectal differences" were defined as any phonological, syntactical, and lexical features manifested by the child that were in current use in the child's cultural community and that also differed from standard English. An effort was made to identify items that existed in the speech of both black and white children.

The acceptance of mountain English and African–American English as distinct and valid linguistic systems by the teachers proved to be the most difficult aspect of this bidialectal program. To promote an understanding of these concepts, several in-service sessions were conducted which attempted to explain previous research and to clarify issues involved in the programs. Three of the Head Start teachers were singled out for further training and instruction in the actual implementation of lesson plans. These teachers were visited at least once a week to eliminate problems, to check on the progress made by the children, and to supply the teachers with new lesson plans. Control and experimental teachers were paired as to their educational background and work experience.

The specific lesson plans for this program were centered around the contrastive analysis approach: A child must (1) recognize that there is a difference between his language and the language he is learning, (2) hear the target language sound or grammatical pattern, (3) discriminate between his language and the target language at the conflict points, (4) reproduce the target language feature, and (5) practice the target language feature in oral drills. The labels of "school" talk and "everyday" talk* were used to differentiate between standard English and the child's dialect.

Special situations were created in order to facilitate the discrimination between "everyday" and "school" talk. Hand puppets, an "everyday" puppet and a "school" puppet, were used in the early stages of the program. Later, pictures that represented a school or everyday environment were presented with the child identifying various speech patterns as appropriate to each. Finally, role playing was instituted; for exam-

---

*A variety of terms have been used interchangeably with "everyday" talk; "other talk," "home talk," and "street talk," in particular, have been widely used as synonyms.

ple, the child could assume the role of mother, father, teacher, or businessman. Varied contexts made the material presented more entertaining for the children and sustained their attention for longer periods of time.

The program was divided into two interrelated phases:

Phase I—a 15-minute formal language instruction period (Monday through Friday) in which the clinician/teacher compared and contrasted the features of the target language with standard English, using the lesson plans previously described

Phase II—reinforcement of the differences between "school" and "everyday" talk by the teacher or her aide at various times throughout the day (primarily in informal situations such as recess or lunch)

Under Phase II the teacher verbally rewarded the child for the appropriate use of school or everyday talk and then asked the child to contrast what had been said with its opposite variety.

Evaluation of the Program

Both statistical evaluation and teacher appraisals confirmed the efficacy of the bidialectal and bicultural training program as compared to the traditional language arts programming. The children used more language and became more expressive in the classroom.

Comment

The utilization of bidialectal strategies incorporated into the Knox County program in conjunction with the more conventional treatment concepts in preschool Head Start programs appears to be desirable. In any innovative, untested program, problems and questions occur, and further research is necessary. The Knox County Program was no exception.

Would a successful bidialectal program be of any relevance for children participating in it? That is, would a command of standard English help a lower-class child to be socially mobile? Some have argued that bidialectalism as an educational program would emotionally harm African–Americans and their groups participating in it and perpetrate an oppression of the lower classes. Although this argument should be considered, there is no proof to substantiate any of the claims. African–American and Appalachian children who become socially mobile tend to "pick up" a certain amount of standard English. This knowledge, however, is not systematic. A bidialectal program, whether at the preschool age or in high school, can make this transition to standard English easier and more thorough.

Analysis of the children's scores suggests that standard English is more effectively learned by poor children when they are taught by the bidialectal–bicultural teaching strategy than by the conventional language arts teaching tool. If the program is to succeed, it is of the utmost importance that before teachers use the bidialectal program they obtain a good understanding of its dynamics and give it their complete support.

The Rosenthal effect (teachers' increased expectations of pupil performance may actually serve to increase pupil performances) was not completely controlled in this experiment. One of the goals, however, was to make teachers more aware of dialect used by children and to show them that it was "different" and not "deficient." Although one of the objectives was to increase teachers' expectancies, at the same time, the changing of teacher attitudes may not by itself be sufficient to guarantee a successful program. A formalized bidialectal program, along with changes in attitudes, seems to be essential.

Is the Daily test an effective measure in evaluating a program of this nature? The Daily measures language used in an artificially created situation—that is, the tester-testee relationship—and may not reflect the natural use of language by the children. Of particular concern is the fact that only a small quantity of speech is produced by the test. This test, in our opinion, is more applicable in measuring language expression than other tests, such as the Peabody Picture Vocabulary Test. Other measures that might be used in future programs are sentence-repetition tests to determine specific use of certain features; tape-recorded samples at school, at play, and at home to ascertain consistent use of either standard English or dialect in different situations; and correlation with standard IQ tests and learning achievement tests to measure any effects of generalization from this program onto scholastic achievement.

A large, extended program needs to be done with equal samples of black and white children. The location of the Knox County study necessitated drawing mainly from white lower-class children. Combined sections of black and white children can be used in similar programs. The clinician or teacher should first determine if any dialectal similarities exist between the groups; then, dialectal differences could be treated in a tridialectal program—that is, special sections where the everyday talk of black and white children is compared and contrasted.

The labels of "everyday" and "school" need to be evaluated in order to determine if, in any way, these connote any racial or superior/inferior distinction. Attitude surveys of both children and teachers before and after the program would be helpful in deciding this question.

An important aspect of any program is the parents. Their attitudes need to be considered and incorporated. Negative parent attitudes can perhaps destroy any program initiated in the school. The clinician or teacher should explain the rationale of the program, and, if necessary, parent-in-service sessions should be conducted to further promote the ideas behind it.

A more definitive evaluation of standard English and nonstandard forms vis-à-vis maturational factors needs to be undertaken than was done in the Knox experiment. The idea age for second-dialect learning needs further investigation. Second-language learning seems to be at optimum strength in the preschool years.

There should be a more rigorous operational definition of standard English, based on the research of socially stigmatized features. Although a precise definition of standard English is nonexistent, a knowledge of what is "nonstandard" is perhaps easier to ascertain. Certain phonological and syntactical features are probably widely viewed as nonstandard and these forms need to be handled in a bidialectal program.

In conclusion, the basic motivation behind the Knox Country program was to make both teachers and children aware that there are dialectal variations in language. By making the study of dialects a part of the language arts curriculum, teachers hopefully do not stereotype children owing to differences in language and children are less intimidated in the preschool classroom because they use their dialect and only secondarily learn the use of another variety, "standard" English. This research showed that children increased their communication skills after bidialectal instruction and showed increased usage of one "standard" English feature, the copula. This program was one of the first to be conducted with predominantly white lower-class Appalachian preschool children. Although there were obvious problems, the initial gains provide an incentive for overcoming any difficulties.

Useful Procedures in a Bidialectal Preschool Program*

On the basis of the experimental Tennessee programs, several procedures can be recommended for a bidialectal preschool program.

To overcome the major difficulty of teaching the concept of "everyday" versus "school" talk to three-year-old children, it is useful to present familiar sounds such as a siren and a school bell and identify them as everyday and school sounds. Similarly, artwork may reflect this distinction by having the children match pictures of "school" with school activities and pictures of "everyday" with everyday-type activities.

Photographs of the classroom and the children's neighborhood may be efficaciously used to suggest school and everyday language concepts rather than drawings or pictures that some of the children may find difficult to relate to. The goal for three-year-old children should be less demanding than for four- and five-year olds; in particular, the former should be expected to develop more acute auditory responsiveness to the distinctions between school and everyday talk, while the latter, hopefully, should also be able to produce verbally some of these distinctions.

The teacher should introduce vocabulary that will become variant. Thus, in the experimental programs when the regular language development lesson plan was concerned with the learning of colors, we suggested that the word *yellow* be taught

---

*Appendixes I and J present other procedures that may be used to implement bidialectal programs.

also in its everyday structure—that is, *yeller*. Although the three-year-old children were not currently saying this variant (or for that matter its school language equivalent) it was very common in their home and peer environment. Therefore, the children would eventually use it.

During the structured phase of the program a brief review of previously learned material should take place so that the children will not forget what transpired in the preceding weeks. Whenever the 10- to 15- minute structured period is determined to be too lengthy (the children become bored), the time spent should be cut to approximately 5 minutes, but the session should be repeated at another time during the day.

Teachers and clinicians should not shy away from emotionally charged words; rather, they should make the children aware that in school there is another way to say these words—that there is a school language equivalent. For example, many of the children use the word "piss"; the distinction was taught that although this is an acceptable everyday form, the school language variant is "go to the bathroom" or "urinate."

There may well be a number of expressions for school or everyday talk. For example, the word "dope" equals everyday talk, while its school talk equivalents are "coke," "soft drink," or "pop." Teachers (and aides) may become more effective language models by using everyday patterns and then "correcting" themselves and saying, "I used an everyday word '——' instead of the school word '——'," thereby allowing the children to hear the contrast and to hear the teacher or aide making the correction. Always indicate that some or most children say "it this way" rather than all children; as a matter of fact, it will be rare for all of the children to use the same everyday pattern, particularly if more than one culture is represented in the class (e.g., poor African–Americans and whites).

Bicultural differences (food, clothes, etc.) need to be incorporated into the program. It is important that cultural institutions, other than language, be compared and contrasted. Differences in clothing styles and food habits, for example, should be taught to the children if such differences exist among the children in a particular classroom. The same strategy used for teaching language differences can be used by the teacher to teach the children about other relevant differences in cultural patterns. Thus, a bidialectal–bicultural teaching program should be developed in racially and socioeconomically integrated classrooms.

Several important factors must be considered in making a bidialectal program successful.

1. Teachers must be instructed in the nature of dialectal differences and should understand the philosophy of bidialectalsim before participation in this program.
2. Teachers in a preschool program should be able to incorporate 15-minute sessions per day into their schedules for bidialectal techniques. The contrastive analysis is an efficient and stimulating method to use with children. Reinforcement of everyday and school talk during the day is essential to the program.

A Sample K–3 Elementary School Program:
A Three-Phase Approach

This section describes the promotion of a bidialectal program in an educational co-operative in rural Tennessee.* Kindergarten through third-grade teachers and their pupils in two schools participated in a specially designed three-phase bidialectal program that lasted for three months. Selected samples of children from each class-room, as well as from control classrooms, were pretested with the Peabody Picture Vocabulary test (PPVT), the Durrell Reading Test (DRT) (Part I), the Daily Language Facility Test (DLFT), and the Mykelbust Picture Story Test (MPST) (Part I). The following material was presented to the participating teachers and discussed with them during an in-service institute.

Rationale   The point of the concept of the bidialectal program is the validity of the speech patterns and behaviors manifested by the children. To suggest to the children that the speech patterns and behaviors used by their parents and friends are improper, as is commonly done, interferes with the learning process.

We believe that a more appropriate approach to the teacher–student interaction is to present middle-class speech patterns (i.e., standard English) and behavioral customs as simply another or different way of talking and behaving and not label native or nonstandard customs as substandard, inferior, or incorrect utterances or behaviors. Thus, the goal is to present to the children the idea that their home or everyday language and behaviors are acceptable and proper in the milieu and that another set of language patterns and behaviors should be used in school—school talk and school behavior. At no time and in no way should their home talk or home behavior be labeled as incorrect. Instead, it is necessary to look upon these construc-tions as being merely different. The teacher must wholeheartedly understand this notion if the bicultural–bidialectal program is to be effective.

Overview   There are three phases to the program: (1) contrastive analysis or aural-oral drill; (2) utilization of lesson plans employing home- and school-talk activities in the classroom; (3) informal promotion of the concept involved during the course of the school day's activities, that is, labeling home talk as home talk when used by a child in response to a question and requesting his school-talk equivalent.

In essence, the program is designed to provide for an equivalent manner of talking and behaving, particularly the former. In traditional programs we label home talk inferior or incorrect; in the bidialectal program we label such utterances "differ-

---

*The actual research was conducted by Ken Clayton as part of his Master's thesis. The re-search was conducted in the Morgan County Public Schools in rural Appalachia.

ent," and we encourage the child to learn both modes of talking but to use them at appropriate times.*

Setting Forth the "Why" of the Program

It is our contention that the lexical differences inherent in mountain and standard English create many learning problems, particularly reading problems, and these problems are more prevalent than heretofore contemplated. By teaching the children these vocabulary equivalencies, we believe it will help them to appreciate better their reading lessons—and hence learn them more successfully.

The phonological and grammatical differences manifested by these children immediately label them as members of a certain culture. In and of itself, this labeling is of no harm; however, when the child becomes an adult and attempts to obtain employment where standard English is desired, the nonstandard speech patterns he or she uses may create an unfavorable image in the mind of the employer. Thus, we want to provide such students with the skills to talk one way when they find it necessary to communicate with members of the "establishment," but encourage them to keep and to use their native dialect when communicating with their peers. In other words, our objective is to make them effective diglossic speakers who can switch dialects.

Presenting the "How"

Phase I   Use of contrastive analysis is Phase I of the program. Three areas comprise the analysis: phonology, grammar, and lexicon. Appropriate examples are recorded on cards for the teacher to use.

The cards for each area contain a contrasting method of saying certain words—all of which are used by most rural Appalachians. For example, on Card 1 you will hear, "Some people say 'across'," followed by "but other people say 'crost'," which is, in turn, followed by, "if some people say 'across'." At this point, a child will be asked to press a button recording his response, which should be, "it means the same as 'crost'." The other children in the class should then be asked if the child's utterance is the proper equivalent. Thus, if the child had happened to record "across," the other children, upon hearing his response, would have noted the fact that he should have used the everyday variant rather than duplicating the school utterance.

There is one set, or two cards, for each construction. Thus, as in the previous example, where we started out with the school language form on the complementary

---

*Obviously there is much redundancy in the presentation of such information. We hope it will be of value to others preparing an in-service program. We gave the teachers a "hand-out" containing the above-noted information and discussed these matters with them in much detail.

card (in this case, Card 2), we start out with the everyday language form and request the school language utterance from the child.

Children should be chosen randomly or by roll, according to teacher preference, and asked to respond to one set each (i.e., the two cards) of the phonological, grammatical, and lexical variants. The children may randomly choose from among the card sets in each of these three sections.

During the first week or two of exposure to this format (or perhaps for the kindergarten and first grades, three or four weeks or more), the child will undoubtedly require help in saying the proper "carrier phrase" ("it means the same as") and the equivalent word (the everyday or school language variant). The other children listening to this process should be encouraged to respond following the child's recording of the word variant; they should not clue the responding child regarding the proper variant to use but should acknowledge the propriety of the response after it has been recorded.

If the child has correctly produced the proper phonological, grammatical, and lexical variants, he should be profusely and meaningfully rewarded. If only one or two of the three presentations produced by the child are correct, he should also be rewarded, but to a lesser degree. The goal is to reinforce the child's understanding of the two variants and their proper use. That is, either construction, everyday or school language, is appropriate and acceptable but only in certain circumstances. The teacher should spend approximately 15 minutes per day on these drills.*

Phase II   In this phase the teacher follows lesson plans employing everyday- and school-talk activities in the classroom. The contrastive analysis program will be of little value unless it can be supplemented by classroom activities designed to encourage proper utilization of the terms. The chapter appendix presents sample lesson plans, all of which employ the plural *s* concept in both everyday and school talk. The teacher may use these, alter them, and/or prepare others as he or she sees fit. Other lesson plans should be created utilizing the same format, or other formats, and involving other word constructions. Approximately 15 minutes per day following the contrastive analysis lesson should be devoted to these exercises.

Phase III   The third phase involves informal promotion of the concept. During the course of the day's activities the teacher should be alert and responsive to the children's use of home language forms. When such an utterance is produced, the teacher may call on another child to note the proper school language variant. Liberal reinforcement should be used.

---

*Note that in our Head Start research programs, we eliminated Phase I and initiated the program with Phase II.

Evaluation of Program

Not only did the children in the program appear to verbalize more effectively but teacher evaluations indicated a plethora of desirable behavior changes in many of the children. Examination of the test data revealed that oral language proficiency increased significantly during the three-month period; the other language forms were not statistically different between pre- and post-test data, but they did show some important trends. In particular, both reading and writing skills appeared to improve in most all the children enrolled in the experimental classes. Of most significance, perhaps, was the teacher appraisal of the program; they commented with much enthusiasm that many of their children demonstrated a lot more participatory behavior in the classroom and that they were, frankly, surprised by the ability level exhibited by some of the children. It is fundamental, of course, that each participant in this program recognize the need for his or her absolute support for the philosophy being espoused. We recognize, as we are sure the reader does, that we have been nurtured by an educational concept propounding the desirability of standard English usage and the substandard nature of other forms. If the teacher maintains this conceptual thinking during interactions in the program, unavoidable harm will be done to the pluralistic concept we are attempting to utilize—which has a history of successful use in our country at different times and in different places.

Conclusion

To the author's knowledge, the experimental Head Start and K–3 programs detailed in this chapter were among the first of their kind in use with lower-class and predominantly white preschool children. There are obvious problems with the bidialectal approach, but the initial gains reported in this research provide an incentive for overcoming any difficulties. The language and culture of the culturally different child need to be respected in our educational system, and a bidialectal program provides an opportunity, as we have repeatedly emphasized, for teachers, clinicians, and children to learn of each other's language and culture.

The investigation of social dialects in American society has received a major impetus since the middle of the 1960s. The major concept emerging from this research is that these varieties of English (black and mountain) are complete linguistic systems in their own right, with specific rules of grammar, phonology, and lexicon, and differ basically in the fact that they are stigmatized or less prestigious forms of standard English. Our research has shown that bidialectal teaching programs can be successfully implemented when this concept is accepted.

Chapter 7 Appendix

Sample Lesson Plans Used in the Knox County (Tennessee) Head Start Bidialectal Training Program

Plan 1

Purposes:

a. To contrast the dialect form "ain't" with the standard English form "isn't."
b. To contrast the vocabulary item "britches" with the standard English forms "pants/slacks."

General Instructions   (may be rephrased every day until the concept is understood):

We talk every day so people can understand what we need. Sometimes we talk different ways when we are in different places. During quiet time we whisper because quiet time is different from other times during the day. Today we're going to learn two kinds of talking, EVERYDAY TALK (place tree on flannel board) and SCHOOL TALK (place school on flannel board).

Everyday Picture: This is our everyday picture. Here are some things we might see every day. We will put our "everyday talk" words with our everyday picture.

School Picture: This is our school picture. Sometimes we talk differently at school. We will put our "school talk" words with our school picture.

Vocabulary to Be Contrasted

Everyday	*School*
ain't	isn't
britches	pants/slacks

Sentences to Be Contrasted

1. She *ain't* cryin'.	vs.	She *isn't* crying.
2. He *ain't* workin'.	vs.	He *isn't* working.
3. He tore his *britches.*	vs.	He tore his *pants/slacks.*
4. My *britches* are brown.	vs.	My *pants/slacks* are brown.

Materials: Level P Peabody Pictures

C-13   P-4   P-24

a. Present everyday word—"ain't."

"Ain't" is an everyday word. It's what we say outside or at home. Teacher gives a picture to a female child in class and says, "She ain't cryin'." Ain't is everyday talk—point to everyday picture.

At school we say "isn't." "Isn't" is school talk. It's how we talk at school. Teacher says, "She isn't crying." Isn't is school talk—point to school picture.

b. Present everyday word—"britches."

"Britches" is everyday talk. Teacher gives picture of britches to a male child in class and says, "He tore his britches." Britches is everyday talk—point to everyday picture.

At school we say pants/ slacks. Pants/slacks is school talk. It's how we talk at school. In school we say, "He tore his pants/slacks." Point to school picture.

c. Proceed with contrasting other sentences.

Variations

1. Receptive task. Present a word verbally in either "everyday" or "school" talk. Have a child point to the picture that the word belongs with.

2. Expressive task. Present a word verbally and ask, "Is this 'school talk' or 'everyday talk'?"

3. Name two puppets "everyday talk" and "school talk." Have "everyday talk" say: If I say, "My britches are brown, what would you say?"

Have "school talk" say, "If you say britches, I would say pants/slacks; my pants/slacks are brown."

Reinforcement   The following reinforcers, which are very important in the learning process, are suggested for use with this program:

1. Present the activity before play time or outside time and as the child responds, allow play to be his reinforcer for responding.

2. Use reinforcers for appropriate responses.

Plan 2

Purpose: To contrast grammatical features and vocabulary items used in standard and nonstandard English.

Vocabulary to be Contrasted

Everyday	School
ain't	doesn't
cheer	chair
no	a

Materials: Level P Peabody Pictures

H-3   P-25   V-8   V-10

Sentences to Be Contrasted

1. He *ain't* got no body.	vs.	He *doesn't* have a body. (V-8)
2. She *ain't* got no friends.	vs.	She *doesn't* have any friends. (P-25)
3. I *ain't* got no head.	vs.	I *don't* have a head. (V-10)
4. The *cheer* is brown.	vs.	The *chair* is brown. (H-3)

Variations

1. Put the children's names in a box (use name cards for name recognition). Teacher will draw a name from the box and the child will identify everyday or school talk:

   a. Receptive task. Present the word verbally and have the child point to the everyday picture or the school picture.

   b. Expressive task. Present the word verbally and ask the child, "Is this school talk or everyday talk?"

2. Have all the children sit on the floor in a circle. Place an empty chair in the middle of the circle. Teacher will say, "(child's name) ain't in the chair," or "(child's name) isn't in the chair," and ask the child, "Is this school talk or everyday talk?" If the child correctly identifies the type of talk, then that child gets to sit in the chair.

Plan 3

Purpose: To contrast grammatical features and vocabulary items used in standard and nonstandard English.

Vocabulary to Be Contrasted

Everyday	*School*
nanner (nana)	banana
yallo (yeller)	yellow
thar	there
brang	brought

Sentences to Be Contrasted

1. This *nanner (nana)* tastes good.	vs.	This *banana* tastes good.
2. The books are over *thar*.	vs.	The books are over *there*.
3. My shirt ain't *yallo (yeller)*.	vs.	My shirt isn't *yellow*.
4. Santa *brang* me a (name of toy).	vs.	Santa *brought* me a (name of toy).

Materials: Level P Peabody Pictures

C-25

T (may use any of the toy pictures)

Banana from the fruit group in the Peabody Kit

Variations

1. Line up the children. Draw a "river" on the floor. Each child asks, "May I cross the river?" Teacher answers, "Yes, if you can tell me if this is school talk or everyday talk." Teacher asks one of the sentences from above or from previous lesson plans. If child misses, he goes to the end of the line.

2. Same as above, but divide into teams. The first team to get all its members across the "river" is the winner.

Plan 4

Purpose: To contrast phonological, grammatical, and lexical items of standard and nonstandard English.

Vocabulary to Be Contrasted

Everyday	*School*
winder	window
this'n	this/this one
spigot	faucet

Sentences to Be Contrasted

1. The *winder* is broken.	vs.	The *window* is broken.
2. *This' n* is mine.	vs.	*This/This one* is mine.*
3. Water comes out of the *spigot*.	vs.	Water comes out of the *faucet*.

*Have the children choose between two objects (or two of the Peabody Level P toy cards). After the child has made a choice, say, "This'n is mine. This'n is everyday talk. Point to the object (card) the child is holding, say, "This is yours (or use child's name). This/this one is school talk."

Variations

1. When the children wash their hands in the bathroom or get a drink of water from the fountain, point out to them that they are washing (drinking) from the spigot (faucet). Have them tell you where the water is coming from; if they use school talk, ask them to tell you the everyday equivalent.

2. Using the Lotto cards provided, call out an everyday (school) word and have the children cover the appropriate box to see if they can identify the word as everyday (school).

Plan 5

Purpose: To contrast phonological, grammatical, and lexical items of standard and nonstandard English.

Materials: Level P Peabody Vocabulary Cards (These cards allow you to present a picture representation of the words.)

A-13   H-2   T-5

or any of the pictures under 70Y Section

Vocabulary to Be Contrasted

Everyday	School
hoss	horse (A-13)
his'n	his (H-2)
fetch	get (T-5)

Sentences to Be Contrasted

1. I rode my *hoss*.	vs.	I rode my *horse*.
2. This cot is *his' n*.	vs.	This cot is *his*.
3. *Fetch* me the crayons (book, etc).	vs.	*Get* me the crayons, etc.

Variations

1. *TRAFFIC SIGNALS*. Give a child two circles, one red, the other green. The red represents everyday talk; the green, school talk. Have the child operate them like traffic signals. The teacher will read an everyday (school) word or sentence while the child stands before the class flashing the red card when he hears everyday talk or the green when he hears school talk. Have the children take turns.

    Vary the game by having the children "cross the street" or "wait at the curb" in response to the red or green signal. The street and curb can be drawn on the floor by chalk lines.

2. Throughout the day, ask the children to "fetch" things, for example at story time, "fetch" the book. If you ask one child to fetch something, ask a different child (1) if that was everyday or school talk; (2) to give the equivalent.

Plan 6

Purpose: To contrast phonological, grammatical, and lexical features of standard and nonstandard English.

Materials: Level P Peabody Vocabulary Cards (These cards allow you to present a visual representation of the vocabulary to be taught.)

F-22 and F-35   T-16   H-1 and H-18

Vocabulary to Be Contrasted

Everyday	School
tater	potato
clum	climbed
pert'n near	almost

Sentences to Be Contrasted

1. I like to eat *tater* chips.   vs.   I like to eat *potato* chips.
2. Momma fixed a baked *tater.*   vs.   Momma fixed a baked *potato.*
3. I *clum* the jungle gym   vs.   I *climbed* the jungle gym
   (monkey bars).   (monkey bars).
4. It's *purt'n near* time for my   vs.   It's *almost* time for my bath
   bath (Sesame Street, etc.).   (Sesame Street, etc.).

Variations

1. Take the children for a walk on the playground. Talk about the everyday things you see—birds, trees, grass, etc. Have each child bring back to class an everyday thing and tell something about it during group time.

2. Teach the children new vocabulary using school tools, for example chalk, eraser, blackboard. Place several items in a row, blindfold a child and remove an item. Take the blindfold off the child and have him name the missing object.

   Do same, using both school and everyday objects. Have the child identify what's missing and tell whether it's an everyday or school item.

Plan 7

Purpose: To contrast phonological, grammatical, and lexical features of standard and nonstandard English.

Materials: Level P Peabody Vocabulary Cards

P-19   P-20   U-15

Vocabulary to Be Contrasted

Everyday	School
fust	first
ketched	caught
packs	carries

Sentences to Be Contrasted

1. The astronaut was the *fust* man   vs.   The astronaut was the *first* man on
   on the moon.   the moon.
2. _____ is *fust* on the bus.   vs.   _____ is *first* on the bus.
3. The leader (name) is *fust* in line.   vs.   The leader (name) is *first* in line.
4. The clown *ketched* the balls.   vs.   The clown *caught* the balls.
5. The bus *packs* children to school.   vs.   The bus *carries* children to school.
6. "_____, *pack* the blocks, etc., to   vs.   "_____, *carry* the blocks, etc., to
   the corner."   the corner."

Variations

1. Set up a restaurant in the classroom. The teacher and aide are waitresses. Have the children order something, using everyday/school talk, that can be eaten for (a) breakfast; (b) lunch; or (c) dinner. (Use the food cards in the Peabody Level P kit.)
2. Use a flannel board to display:
   a. One picture of an everyday item and one picture of a school item: Point to one of the pictures, have a child find one just like it; and/or tell if it is an everyday or school picture.
   b. Three pictures, two of which are everyday and one of which is school: Have the child point to the one that is different and/or identify if it is school or everyday.

Plan 8: Review

In addition to the general review that occurs each week, a more comprehensive review of *all* vocabulary items should take place. Therefore, it is recommended that *every fourth week* be devoted to a review of *all* vocabulary taught to date.

A suggestion for review is to let the children select their favorite card from among those used with the lesson plans and then talk about it using everyday (school) talk. Using school talk, the teacher can label the sentence for the child, then ask the child if he or she can say the same thing using everyday talk.

You are also encouraged to be creative. Develop new sentences rather than use the ones presented with the lesson plans.

Vocabulary

Everyday	School
got	have
gots	has
ain't	isn't

britches	pants/slacks
ain't got no	doesn't have a
cheer	chair
nanner (nana)	banana
yallo (yeller)	yellow
thar	there
brang	brought
purty	pretty
'posed	supposed
follerin'	following
poke	bag/paper bag
a'goin'/goin'	going
pocketbook	purse
winder	window
this'n	this/this one
spigot	faucet

Plan 9

Purpose: To contrast vocabulary and pronunciation items of standard and non-standard English.

Materials: Peabody Level P Vocabulary Cards

F-34   U-16   C-27

Vocabulary to Be Contrasted

Everyday	*School*
poke	bag/paper bag (F-34)
a'goin/goin	going (U-16)
pocketbook	purse (C-27)

Sentences to Be Contrasted

1. (Child's name) has a *poke* of popcorn.	vs.	(Child's name) has a *bag* of popcorn.
2. The bus is *a'goin'/goin* to school.	vs.	The bus is *going* to school.
3. Teacher has a *pocketbook.*	vs.	Teacher has a *purse.*

Variations

1. Label two paper bags "poke" and "bag." Put an everyday picture on the poke and a school picture on the bag. Have the children put everyday things in the poke and school things in the bag.

2. Have some of the children draw an everyday picture and some draw a school picture. Then ask the children to talk about what they have drawn.

Plan 10

Purpose: To contrast phonological, grammatical, and lexical items of standard and nonstandard English.

Materials: Level P Peabody Vocabulary Cards (These cards allow you to present a picture representation of the words.)

A-37   T-26   P-18

Vocabulary to Be Contrasted

Everyday	*School*
wasper	wasp (A-37)
drawed	drew (T-26)
tuckered-out	tired (P-18)

Sentences to Be Contrasted

1. The *wasper* stung me.	vs.	The *wasp* stung me.
2. He/she *drawed* this cat.	vs.	He/she *drew* this cat.
3. Teacher is all *tuckered out*.	vs.	Teacher is *tired*.

Variations

1. Pin a picture representing school (everyday) talk on each child. The teacher says, "All those children who are school talk go sit on the rug; all those children who are everyday talk go to the table." This can be used when moving from a large group activity, dividing into small group activities.

2. Have all the school talk children go to one side of the room and the everyday talk children to the other side of the room. The teacher asks, "How many school talk children do we have today? How many everyday talk children do we have at school today? Are there more school talk children than everyday talk children?

3. Place three items on the flannelboard, for example two everyday pictures and one school picture. Ask the children (a) to point to the one that is different; and (b) to name the one that is different.

Plan 11

Purpose: To contrast prosodic features of standard and nonstandard English.

The prosodic features—rhythm, melody, rate and stress (force)—make language more expressive. Syllables and words can be compared to an accordion—they can be stretched out or compressed. In speech, some utterances are "drawn out" to express contentment, weariness, reverence, awe, or deep grief. Utterances may also be compressed to express an extreme emotional state—fear, rage, or excitement.

Nonstandard English may be characterized by slow, quiet timing in speech with pause between syllables and words. In standard English, these pauses may create an uncomfortable feeling in the listener and/or speaker.

To help the children become more aware of these contrasts, demonstrate and contrast fast and slow rhythms through clapping, beating drums, tapping, marching, walking, etc. Talk about the differences as you demonstrate the rhythms. Perhaps the teacher could demonstrate one form (e.g., fast) and her aide, the other (e.g., slow). Demonstrate them, then have the children repeat them. Have the children do them with you.

Vocabulary to Be Contrasted

Everyday	*School*
1. Counting: o-n-e, t-wo, th-r-ee . . .	one, two, three
2. Sa- a- a- ad	sad
3. N - o- o- o	no

Variations

1. Ask a child to count the other children in the circle using everyday (school) talk. Ask the remaining children whether he/she used everyday (school) talk.

2. As the children go from group time to another activity, explain to them that they have a choice between two activities. To get to the next activity, they must ask the teacher (aide), "May I go to the _____?" If they do not ask "May I," the teacher (aide) will respond using the everyday (school) form "No (n-o-o-o) you cannot go to the _____."

   On the playground, line the children up to play "May I." The teacher (aide) can be "IT." The children must ask "May I take two small steps?," etc. If children say "May I," they are allowed to take the steps, etc. If not, the reply is "No (n-o-o) you may not take _____." First child to reach "IT" becomes the new "IT."

3. Select a child from the group and ask him/her to put on a "Happy Face." Ask the other children, "Is _____ sad (sa-a-ad)? Have them reply using everyday (school) talk, "No (no-o-o), _____ isn't sad (sa-a-ad).

   Dress the children up. Explain that they are going to town to grocery shop. The teacher (aide) may be the clerk. The children go into the store and ask, "Do you have any _____ for sale?" The clerk will reply, "No (No-o-o), I don't have any _____ for sale." Let the children take turns being the clerk, explaining to them they must use the everyday (school) talk way to say "NO."

Plan 12: Review

Vocabulary to Be Contrasted

Everyday Talk	*School Talk*
got	have
gots	has
ain't	isn't
britches	pants/slacks
ain't got no	doesn't have a
cheer	chair
nanner (nana)	banana
yallo (yeller)	yellow
thar	there
brang	brought
purty	pretty
'posed	supposed
follerin'	following
poke	bag/paper bag
a'goin'/goin'	going
pocketbook	purse
winder	window
this'n	this/this one
spigot	faucet
hoss	horse
his'n	his
fetch	get
wasper	wasp
drawed	drew
tuckered out	tired

Sentences to Be Contrasted

1. I *got* me some new shoes.   vs.   I *have* some new shoes.
2. My daddy *gots* a motorcycle.   vs.   My daddy *has* a motorcycle.
3. _____ *ain't* here today.   vs.   _____ *isn't* here today.
4. My *britches* are torn.   vs.   My *pants/slacks* are torn.
5. Teacher *ain't got no* crayons.   vs.   Teacher *doesn't have any* crayons.
6. The *cheer* is broken.   vs.   The *chair* is broken.
7. I like *nanners* on my cereal.   vs.   I like *bananas* on my cereal.
8. The sun is *yallo (yeller)*.   vs.   The sun is *yellow*.
9. She *brang* the note home.   vs.   She *brought* the note home.
10. _____ has a *purty* new dress, etc.   vs.   _____ has a *pretty* new dress, etc.

11. You not *'posed* to hit.	vs.	You're not *supposed* to hit.
12. The policeman is *follerin'* that car.	vs.	The policeman is *following* that car.
13. I put my candy in a *poke*.	vs.	I put my candy in a *bag/paper bag*.
14. The bus is *a' goin/goin* to school.	vs.	The bus is *going* to school.
15. Ladies carry *pocketbooks*.	vs.	Ladies carry *purses*.
16. My momma washed the *winder*.	vs.	My momma washed the *window*.
17. I'm going to color with *this' n*.	vs.	I'm going to color with *this one*.
18. I got a drink of water from the *spigot*.	vs.	I got a drink of water from the *faucet*.
19. A *hoss* lives on a farm.	vs.	A *horse* lives on a farm.
20. That coat is *his' n*.	vs.	That coat is *his*.
21. The *wasper* built a nest.	vs.	The *wasp* built a nest.
22. I *drawed* me a house.	vs.	I *drew* a house.
23. I'm all *tuckered out* from running.	vs.	I'm *tired* from running.

8

Nonnative Language: Its Assessment and Management

Assessment of Language Proficiency

During the past decade a variety of studies have been published that express diverse viewpoints regarding the role of the speech–language specialist (SLS) with limited-English-proficient (LEP) speakers (e.g., Alterbaum and Buck 1982; Brand 1981; Dreher 1981; Gandour 1980; Gillcrist 1981; Kayser 1989; Koening and Biel 1989; MacKay 1978; Peins, Colburn, and Goetz 1984; Weiner, Bergen, and Bernstein 1983). Most of these publications support the concept that our role is to help these individuals *use* English effectively. *But another neglected and challenging role that the SLS can play pertains to the assessment of the language proficiency of these speakers as it relates to their normal or special class placement.* Our profession can and should significantly contribute to proficiency issues, and we should accomplish this task by participating as members of the educational team that traditionally assesses language proficiency.

The reality of the current situation, however, is that most SLSs are unprepared to provide the additional information because of four major obstacles: (1) lack of sufficient or appropriate academic preparation; (2) unfamiliarity with the cultural and linguistic differences of LEP children; (3) lack of experience in interacting with such speakers; (4) lack of appropriate assessment tools. But the need to overcome these obstacles is evident if we are to provide a needed service to these children. Therefore, it is important for SLSs to obtain the requisite preparation and to make known their desire to serve on assessment teams evaluating language proficiency. To obtain the appropriate knowledge, our training institutions must provide students and practicing professionals relevant cultural and linguistic information and appropriate assessment and management experiences. As noted by Mattes and Omark (1984), few academic programs provide the training to enable the SLS to perform comprehensive language assessments of LEP students.

Assessment of the LEP Child

Language minority children or the LEP usually perform at lower academic levels as compared to majority children, the standard-English-speaking children (Rueda et al. 1985). Thus, some children may be placed in special education classes because of their limited English proficiency, whereas other children may be placed in inappropriate regular classrooms and may manifest unsatisfactory progress owing to their limited command of the English language. Appropriate identification and assessment of language skills and proper academic placement are obviously of critical importance if these children are to perform adequately. Rueda et al. (1985) suggest that the proficiency instruments utilized by the assessment teams do not generate sufficient information relevant to the demands of the classroom.

Additional assessment measures must be supplied that will enable the team to determine if the aural–oral limited English used by LEP children is appropriate for their class placement. These measures will also determine whether the children possess deficiencies in their communication skills. This is particularly the case with LEP children who may not be performing adequately in the regular or special classrooms. SLSs may be able to supply the additional assessment information.

A Proposed Assessment Instrument

This chapter presents an assessment instrument (see the chapter appendix) that can be used by the SLS when evaluating the aural–oral language proficiency of LEP (or nonstandard dialect) speakers of English. The instrument obtains, in addition to this proficiency measure, information regarding any deficiencies in the student's native language (or dialect). The assessment instrument also incorporates information relevant to nonlinguistic behaviors such as prosodic and body language patterns.

The basis of the evaluation is the recorded informal language samples obtained in at least two (but preferably three) situations, and if possible with different examiners. Playbacks of these tape-recorded samples should reveal to the tester the level of pragmatic English language usage available to the LEP student plus the detection of any disordered speech–language patterns. Such an instrument, we believe, is more valid than many conventional standardized tests. The norm for these conventional tests cannot appropriately be applied to the various ethnic, racial, and socio-economically different students. In addition to the assessment instrument, some pragmatic tests of language that can be used by either the SLS or the teacher are given in the following sections of this chapter.

Listening and Speaking Tests of Language

Intelligible and effective communication is the foundation for achievement in school. Thus the ability to identify, assess, and place nonnative or LEP speakers of English in academic classes commensurate with their level of English language proficiency is of pressing importance. Or, as Fradd, Barona, and DeBaron (1989, p. 73) state, "Training in language assessment is important in ensuring that students receive the educational assistance and the language input that they require to become successful." This is particularly important with children who receive special education services.

Oral Language Proficiency Testing

As noted previously, joint assessments by the SLS and the various teachers, particularly the teachers of English to speakers of other languages (TESOL)* personnel, are desirable. The TESOL teacher (or others) can administer a psychoeducational battery of tests that will help determine the academic strengths and weaknesses of the students, as well as give some information about their verbal and performance skills. But it is only when the SLS assesses such children's communication skills that definitive information regarding the aural–oral bilingual proficiency level of the students can be obtained. Since these limited-English-speaking children from different racial, ethnic, and social groups are not from homogenous cultures, no one standardized test is generally appropriate to all of them. Even discrete bilingual speakers such as Spanish-speaking or Spanish–English-speaking children may have been reared in different linguistic cultures; thus, for example, the Mexican–American, the Central– or South– or Cuban–American, and the Puerto Rican–American all speak somewhat different dialects of Spanish.

Therefore, analysis of language samples obtained from the LEP speaker, as well as one's diagnostic–clinical experience, may be an appropriate and important adjunctive basis for the proficiency evaluation (Kayser 1989). Obtaining information about students' aural–oral language proficiency as well as the determination of whether speech–language–hearing disorders exist is useful information for an educational assessment team.

---

*Some writers use the TESOL abbreviation (see Gandour 1980), but others may use TOSEL (see Weiner, Bergen, and Bernstein 1983).

An Overview of the Assessment Dynamics

A cursory examination of language proficiency tests demonstrates that most evaluate one or another of the segmentals of language use—that is, the phonemes, vocabulary, and/or grammar (Damico 1985). Evaluation of a child's pragmatic uses of language in different contexts, particularly the school contexts, are infrequent (Fradd, Barona, and DeBaron 1989). Furthermore, examination of suprasegmental and body language patterns used in the classroom seem to be virtually ignored. Much of the debating in the past twenty years regarding the relationship between language proficiency and academic achievement has failed to take into account these distinctions.

The many tests of language proficiency seem to have poor validity for both school placement as well as the many facets of informal and interpersonal language use. Insofar as the former point is concerned, Jax (1988) discusses recent research with Hispanic children who passed conventional language proficiency examinations and were placed in regular classrooms but who subsequently failed their academic coursework. These children were subsequently referred to special education classes because of their poor reading and oral language skills as well as their low academic achievement in the regular classroom. These findings clearly support the contention that conventional oral language proficiency testing leaves much to be desired; too many children are being misplaced (e.g., Mercer 1976). Thus, the use of listening and speaking tests of language as presented in Figure 8-1 is very desirable. The SLS can enhance the accurate assessment of an LEP student's ability to understand and use appropriate spoken English in different situations through such a testing format. Test information obtained by the SLS can also give support to any second language teaching program. Such data may provide important insights into all aspects of a student's language proficiency, in all language skills, and can be indispensable guides in helping to place the student in an appropriate class and instructional level. They can also help teachers plan the language curriculum and each class lesson so that the particular needs of each student will be met.

Figure 8-1 Pragmatic Tests of Language [From English Language Resource Center, Center for Applied Linguistics, Arlington, VA (1984). Some changes in context and format have been made.]

Listening Tests

1. Type: **Phonological Discrimination**

Purpose: To test students' ability to recognize and compare
a. Sounds (may use Wepman test)
b. Intonation contours
c. Stress

Example: Teacher reads contrastive or similar units and asks students to state whether the elements they heard were the same or different, question vs. statement, intonation emphatic vs. normal stress, and so forth.

2. Type: **Appropriate Response**

Purpose: To test students' ability to respond appropriately in an oral message.

Example: Teacher reads: What did you think of the soccer game?

Student responds to one of the following:
a. It was the most boring game I ever saw.
b. I thought of the game.
c. It was the most boring game I ever went.

3. Type: **Global Comprehension**

Purpose: To test students' ability to hear a small segment of discourse and make global inferences as to where the conversation took place.

Example: Teacher reads: How much is the lettuce? Do they sell rice? Let's ask the manager. Where does this conversation take place?

Student responds to one of the following:
a. It's a nice place.
b. In a supermarket.
c. In an airline office.

4. Type: **Statement Rejoinder**

Purpose: To check students' ability to respond with an appropriate rejoinder to an oral stimulus.

Example: Teacher reads: Would you mind if I took your plate now?

Student responds to one of the following:
a. Yes, I am finished eating.
b. Yes, I haven't finished yet.
c. No, I am still eating.
d. No, I haven't finished yet.

(continues)

Figure 8-1 *Continued*

---

5. Type: **Completion**

Purpose: To verify students' ability to complete logically an utterance presented orally.

Example: Teacher reads: I'm hungry.

Student responds to one of the following:
a. Where is the bank?
b. Where can I get something to drink?
c. Where is the bathroom?
d. Where is the nearest restaurant?

6. Type: **Same–Different**

Purpose: To test students' ability to differentiate between grammatical or lexical forms.

Example: Indicate whether the pairs of statements that follow are the same or different by telling *S* (same) or *D* (different) on the line provided:

1. ___ He's not old enough to drive.
He's too young to drive.
2. ___ He's hardly working.
He's working hard.
3. ___ He could have helped.
He might have helped.
4. ___ He could not have said that.
He might not have said that.
5. ___ He must not go now.
He doesn't have to go now.

Speaking Tests

---

1. Type: **Directed Dialogues**

Purpose: To test students' ability to create natural conversations with a minimum of errors and a fair degree of fluency.

Format: Teacher reads or students read a brief incident from which they have to create a dialogue.

Situation: A young man, dressed in jeans, is being questioned by a clerk in an employment office.

2. Type: **The Telephone Game**

Purpose: To check students' understanding of roles and functions in the target culture. Moreover, this activity checks students' ability to ask questions.

Figure 8-1 *Continued*

Format: Teacher asks students to pretend to telephone the following places:
a. Police department
b. Employment office
c. Fire department
d. Restaurant
e. School

3. Type: **Directed Disclosure**

Purpose: To evaluate students' ability to ask questions in English.

Format: (To student A):
a. Ask student B if he's ever eaten spaghetti.
b. Ask him if he liked it.
c. Ask him where he ate it.
d. Ask him what it tasted like.

Variation: The teacher knows an individual in the class who has done something "unusual" recently. He/she encourages other students to generate questions about his/her "achievement."

Examples:
a. Trip to Montana
b. Visit to the Grand Canyon, New York, and so forth.

4. Type: **Games/Variation**

Purpose: To check students' ability to formulate questions in English.

Format: By using the format of such games as:
a. What's My Line?
b. Twenty Questions
c. I've Got a Secret

The teacher can evaluate the students' questioning strategies.

5. Type: **Interview**

Purpose: To check students' ability to generate questions and to expand appropriately upon information given.

Format: Student is given a blank application form (for credit or employment). He/she is then directed to ask questions in order to complete the application form.

6. Type: **Role Plays**

Purpose: To check students' ability to describe what they see in clear and accurate English and to communicate that description to another person effectively.

Format: Teacher gives student A a picture which student A must describe to student B. Student B tries to draw what he hears. At the end of the task, student A and student B compare pictures.

(continues)

Figure 8-1 *Continued*

---

7. **Type:**   **Giving Directions/Map Skills**

    Purpose: To check students' ability to give clear and accurate directions.

    Format: Teacher provides students with maps or a wall map/poster may be used.

    Task: Student is to describe how to get from location A to location B.

8. **Type:**   **Outlines**

    Purpose: To check students' ability to expand brief sentences into more complicated ones.

    Format: Students are given an outline on which they must expand.

9. **Type:**   **Guided Speaking**

    Purpose: To check students' ability to communicate effectively in English; to make descriptions, to report feelings, and so on.

    Task: Have students describe a meal they had in a restaurant, a movie they have seen, or an occasion in their life when they felt they were in danger.

NOTE: At all times evaluate carefully the client's/student's use of prosody and body language. If differences are noted, compare/contrast with standard English.

Assessment Issues

The Reliability of Our Test Data

The Monolingual–Monodialectal Assessor   According to the *Education of All Handicapped Children Act* (1975), tests and testing procedures must not be racially or culturally discriminating. Yet misclassifications and subsequent misplacement of nonstandard, nonnative, and limited speakers of English (or non-English proficient [NEP] children and LEP children) appear to be quite common despite the safeguards inherent in PL 94–142 and other laws. For example, the earlier *Lau v. Nichols* 1974 Supreme Court decision stated that standardized tests administered by monolingual speakers to culturally diverse (C.D.) testees are often unfair and biased. Does this apply to nonstandard-speaking clients and standard-speaking testers? It clearly applies to NEP/LEP clients and English-speaking testers. Yet, because of the preponderance of monolingual–monodialectal testers, we probably violate this law during much of our testing of multicultural clients. How should we pragmatically cope with this problem?

Examiner Familiarity Is there any difference in testee performance when the degree of familiarity between the tester–testee is (1) well developed, (2) casual, or (3) essentially minimal? According to Fuchs and Fuchs (1989), "Black and Hispanic children scored significantly *and dramatically* higher with familiar examiners" (italics added). Since tester unfamiliarity is the rule rather than the exception in many of our programs, this clearly contributes to "a spuriously low performance of minority children and increases the likelihood that they will be identified inaccurately as handicapped" (p. 304).

Thus as noted in previous chapters, when assessing C.D. clients we must address the familiarity issue. An effort should be made to ensure the existence of an adequate and relaxed relationship when testing such children.

Bilingual Testing The NEP/LEP child may or may not be disordered in his or her own language (as well as in English). Thus, appropriate testing is required in the child's native language as well as in English. Such dual testing precipitates the following questions.

1. How does English differ from the child's native communication system? That is, what differences are there in phonology, lexicon, grammar, pragmatics, prosody, body language? For example, which English speech sounds have no counterpart in the native language? Which English sounds are similar to the native sounds but are not the same?

2. How do we distinguish between disorder and difference in the native language?* As David Yoder (1970) voiced in his insightful chapter in the book *Language and Poverty,* "The type of distinction between deficit and difference carries weighty implications . . . ."

3. How do we obtain, train and pay qualified interpreters to assist with the evaluation? If the evaluator is monolingual, the services of a testing aide should be obtained. The aide must be a person who is knowledgeable of the client's culture, is conversant in his or her language dialect, and can appropriately administer tests.

The Validity of Our Test Data

Standardized Tests Standardization criteria of normative tests must be representative of the various cultures (racial, ethnic, and social class groups) and regions of

---

*In addition to the native language (L1) and acquired language (L2) there is the dialectal English that the child uses in his everyday activities. For example, Hispanic speakers from the Southwest often employ "Tex-Mex," a variant of English and Mexican Spanish, to communicate.

this country if they are to be valid. Many of our normed tests however, do not use many representative cultural and regional samples. The reason is simple: such standardizing of tests becomes prohibitive in terms of cost, time, and effort. Because of the difficulties involved in standardizing tests for all multicultural clients, we must question the validity of the test information we obtain from culturally different children for the following reasons:

1.   The scores of the culturally diverse children will generally be lower than those achieved by middle-class children taking conventional standardized tests. These lower scores are to be expected since many of the tests were standardized on middle-class children. As an example, the original Peabody Picture Vocabulary Test, in our judgment, caused an approximate 20-point differential in scores to occur in children from different social classes. Note that this test was normed on middle-class white children from Nashville, Tennessee. How we interpret this differential is of crucial importance. For example:

2.   Such lowered scores may allow for lowered expectations; the Rosenthal or Pygmalion effect—what you expect is what you get—may well be precipitated by these depressed scores. What then should we do? Should we renorm the test for our particular speech community?

Renorming the Test   When attempting to eliminate or reduce bias by renorming the test because of inappropriate or insufficient standardization controls as just discussed, one should be cognizant that such renorming may create a variety of problems such as the following:

1.   If we renorm the test and create a culture-fair test, is the data obtained relevant to the needs of the classroom teacher? To the SLS? Might a culturally biased test be more appropriate to the needs of teacher or clinician if it is correctly interpreted? What, then, are we supposed to do?

2.   Are both culturally fair (from peer groups in their local speech communities) and culturally biased (from middle-class standardized norms) test results desirable? If so, should we obtain both sets of information? Is this practical?

Identity of Paralinguistic Patterns

There is a need to include both language suprasegmentals as well as body language in the testing procedures in order to obtain a valid "picture" or profile of a child's nonstandard or nonnative communicative patterns. Since aspects of an utterance convey approximately 93 percent of the *impact* of a message transmission (Mehrabian 1969), it is important that we distinguish between the standard paralinguistic patterns and the nonstandard or nonnative behaviors during our assessment procedures. But, we would hazard a guess that any attempts to obtain such data are relatively infrequent and that little attention is paid to these factors in our test reports.

Management Issues

The Three Different Student Populations

We may want to interact with three different student populations: (1) The multicultural exceptional client with communication disorders; (2) the multicultural essentially normal client with speech–language disorders who is currently treated in our clinical programs; as well as (3) the multicultural normal speaker *without speech–language disorders*, but who is not typically served by SLSs. Shouldn't there be a cooperative interaction between SLSs and teachers of English and a second language (TESL)? For example, Peins, Colburn, and Goetz (1984) suggest normal LEP students be taught all the oral segmentals of English: articulation, vocabulary, grammar (both syntax and morphology), and pragmatic use of language, as well as the suprasegmentals and body language. To do this effectively requires specialized interactions with the TESL people.

The Public School Populations

Gillcrist (1981) presents a justifiable rationale for including normal LEP students in the public school clinician's caseloads. Is this being done in our schools? Also, some school districts apparently admit to therapy only children who have disorders *in both* the native language and in English, while other school districts allow into therapy children whose disorder is in the native language only, *or* in English, *or* in both languages. What impact does this have on our public school's speech therapy programs?

Conclusion

Clearly, one of the more pressing and potentially divisive areas of disagreement among speech–language specialists, teachers of English to speakers of other languages, resource teachers, classroom teachers, and teachers of English is the appropriate assessment of communicative proficiency. The Assessment Instrument for Multicultural Clients given in the chapter appendix is designed to provide the appropriate assessment for multicultural students.

The Multicultural Assessment Test

As previously noted, the test is designed to be used on either nonstandard or nonnative speakers of English. Directions for its use are given on the front page of the test, as is identification information. The following page of the assessment instrument allows the examiner to determine if all the test data have been accomplished; this in turn is followed by a summary of results form. Note that the results are scaled from normal, or appropriate, to abnormal, or inappropriate.

The test itself starts on the fourth page of the instrument. The following communicative aspects are to be evaluated.

1. Speech intelligibility. The tester evaluates how understandable the child is. The goal is to determine whether there are difficulties due to his or her dialect.
2. Amount of dialect or language difference. The tester estimates, on a 5-point scale, the amount of dialect and/or language differences manifested in each of the five components of language, plus an overall estimate.
3. Use of suprasegmentals (the prosody of language), body language (or the body kinesics), voice patterns, and fluency patterns. The test items for each of these areas include space for the tester to record unusual observations in addition to the listed behaviors and patterns.
4. Auditory comprehension, plus morphologic, syntactic, and grammar problems. These areas are scaled by the tester in the last part of the test.

A form is available (last page of the instrument) for the classroom teacher to use. It contains much of the previously noted information but is related specifically to classroom communicative behavior, both verbal and nonverbal, of LEP children.

If public school SLSs and teachers are to have effective and efficient interactions with such nonnative or LEP speakers, there must be an awareness that the differing mores, cognitive patterns, and particularly the linguistic behaviors manifested by such students require input from all these professional workers. Thus, a multidisciplinary assessment in both the native and acquired mores, patterns, and behaviors is desirable.

Summary Statement

According to conventional estimates, there will be a very significant increase of multicultural students in our schools in the next decade and beyond (Ramirez 1988; Weiner, Bergen, and Bernstein 1983). These authors note that the increase will greatly expand the numbers of Asian Americans, Pacific Islanders, Native Americans (both Alaskan and Plains), and most particularly, Hispanics in our country. By the turn of the century, according to Ramirez (1988, p. 45), ". . . it is projected that 40 percent of public school students will be from these and other ethnically diverse backgrounds." It is quite apparent that members of the teaching and helping professions need to become psychologically and socially sensitized to differing cultural mores and both educationally and clinically sophisticated regarding the different cognitive and linguistic behaviors unique to members of these different cultures. Unless we are aware of the unique differences, problems, and concerns of the increasing number of multicultural students in our schools, we shall be ill equipped to cope with their needs.

Chapter 8 Appendix

ASSESSMENT INSTRUMENT FOR MULTICULTURAL CLIENTS   **1**

Client's Name: _____

Age:_____ Sex:_____ School Grade:_____

1. Evaluator of L1* _____ Date_____
                             (name of SLS or Interpreter)†

    If Interpreter, check whether: Family Member _____ Other_____

2. Evaluator of L2†† _____Date_____
                                  (name of SLS)

3. Evaluator of Dialect _____ Date_____
                                  (name of SLS)

Nonnative English Speaker	*Nonstandard English Speaker*
1. Spanish Influenced English _____	**4.** African Influenced English_____
2. Asian Influenced English _____	**5.** Appalachian Influenced English _____
3. Other _____	**6.** Other _____

UTILIZATION OF THE ASSESSMENT INSTRUMENT

1. The following assessment instrument can be used to evaluate the communicative proficiency of both LEP as well as nonstandard speakers of English. In particular, this model allows for the determination and recording of a client's (1) linguistic deficiencies vs. differences, (2) appropriate vs. inappropriate use of language, and (3) the quantity of nonnative or nonstandard English utterances.

2. At a minimum, obtain at least two relatively short language samples; if possible, obtain three samples in different situations.

3. Play back the language samples as frequently as is necessary in order to obtain the relevant information concerning the student's communication skills. As you do so, listen intently for each facet of the assessment instrument.

4. If necessary or desired, you may use a standardized test, particularly an articulation test of your choice, to supplement the information obtained through the language samples.

---

*L1 = Native Language

†SLS = Speech–Language Specialist

††L2 = Acquired Language/English

2

AURAL/ORAL COMMUNICATIVE ASSESSMENTS

Check if
Accomplished

_____ 1. Pragmatic Language Samples: Obtain samples of language usage in at least two different situations and, if possible, with two different testers in each of the situations. Note and discuss the following:

_____   A. Clinic: intelligibility of the sample ....page 4a and the quantity of dialect/language differences ....page 4b

     B. Other: compare to clinic sample

_____ 2. Evaluate client's use of segmentals. By subjective or objective testing, note and discuss the phonological and morphosyntactic utterances you observe that are inappropriate for the language/dialect being assessed. See morphosyntactic summary ....page 6

_____ 3. Evaluate client's use of suprasegmentals and body language ....page 4c

_____ 4. Evaluate client's voice and fluency patterns ....page 4d

_____ 5. Evaluate client's auditory acuity and comprehension ....page 5e

_____ 6. Use of Language in the Classroom (if appropriate). Ascertain from teacher: ....page 7

     (1) intelligibility of the speaker;

     (2) amount of dialect/language differences used by child;

     (3) his/her knowledge and use of standard language rules in the classroom;

     (4) the child's auditory comprehension in L1 and L2.

SUMMARY OF RESULTS   **3**

Circle the Appropriate Number

	Nonnative Language Speaker		Nonstandard Dialect Speaker
	Native Language	English	
	(specify)		(specify)
1. Pragmatic Usage	I_I_I_I_I * 1 2 3 4 5	I_I_I_I_I 1 2 3 4 5	I_I_I_I_I 1 2 3 4 5
Intelligibility	I_I_I_I_I 1 2 3 4 5	I_I_I_I_I 1 2 3 4 5	I_I_I_I_I 1 2 3 4 5
Quantity of Overall Language/Dialect Differences	I_I_I_I_I 1 2 3 4 5	I_I_I_I_I 1 2 3 4 5	I_I_I_I_I 1 2 3 4 5
2. Segmentals Phonology	I_I_I_I_I 1 2 3 4 5	I_I_I_I_I 1 2 3 4 5	I_I_I_I_I 1 2 3 4 5
Grammar	I_I_I_I_I 1 2 3 4 5	I_I_I_I_I 1 2 3 4 5	I_I_I_I_I 1 2 3 4 5
Vocabulary	I_I_I_I_I 1 2 3 4 5	I_I_I_I_I 1 2 3 4 5	I_I_I_I_I 1 2 3 4 5
3. Suprasegmentals and Body Language	I_I_I_I_I 1 2 3 4 5	I_I_I_I_I 1 2 3 4 5	I_I_I_I_I 1 2 3 4 5
4. Voice and Fluency Patterns	I_I_I_I_I 1 2 3 4 5	I_I_I_I_I 1 2 3 4 5	I_I_I_I_I 1 2 3 4 5

5. Audition

Acuity—	passed screening	____	____
	failed screening	____	____
Comprehension Acceptable	____	____	____
Unacceptable and below expectations	____	____	____

6. Use of Language in the Classroom (if school age child):
Acceptable____   Unacceptable and below expectations____

*I_I_I_I_I
1 2 3 4 5

1 = Appropriate or normal response; in the case of the quantity of language/dialect differences it refers to minimal or no differences.

5 = The most inappropriate or abnormal response—the most severe; in the case of the language/dialect differences it refers to the maximal difference.

4

FOR THE SPEECH–LANGUAGE SPECIALIST

Native Language (L1), Acquired English (L2), Nonstandard Dialect (D)

(a) INTELLIGIBILITY

L1 L2 D

___ ___ ___ **1.** Standard pronunciation, with no trace of "different" accent or dialect.

___ ___ ___ **2.** No conspicuous mispronunciations but would not be taken for a native speaker because of some subtle prosodic differences.

___ ___ ___ **3.** Marked accent and occasional mispronunciations which do not interfere with understanding.

___ ___ ___ **4.** Accent or prosody not appropriate to dialect/language being assessed and leading to occasional misunderstanding.

___ ___ ___ **5.** Frequent gross errors and a very heavy accent making understanding difficult.

(b) AMOUNT OF DIALECT/LANGUAGE DIFFERENCES NOTED WHEN SPEAKER IS USING "STANDARD" ENGLISH

Estimate the amount of dialect/language differences on the following scales (minimum or none to maximum) (Circle the appropriate number.)

Phonology	Grammar	Vocabulary	Prosody	Body Language	Overall
1 2 3 4 5	1 2 3 4 5	1 2 3 4 5	1 2 3 4 5	1 2 3 4 5	1 2 3 4 5

(c) SUPRASEGMENTALS OR PROSODY

L1 L2 D

___ ___ ___ **1.** Appropriate

___ ___ ___ **2.** Stress pattern is unusual*

___ ___ ___ **3.** Intonation pattern is unusual

___ ___ ___ **4.** Inflection pattern is unusual

___ ___ ___ **5.** Loudness pattern is unusual

___ ___ ___ **6.** Pitch pattern is unusual

___ ___ ___ **7.** Other_____

BODY LANGUAGE

L1 L2 D

___ ___ ___ **1.** Appropriate

___ ___ ___ **2.** Eye contact pattern is unusual

___ ___ ___ **3.** Eye movement pattern is unusual

___ ___ ___ **4.** A body movement pattern is unusual

___ ___ ___ **5.** Spacial relationship is unusual

___ ___ ___ **6.** Other_____

(d) VOICE PATTERNS

L1 L2 D

___ ___ ___ **1.** Appropriate

___ ___ ___ **2.** Harshness seems to be abnormal*

___ ___ ___ **3.** Breathiness seems to be abnormal

___ ___ ___ **4.** Loudness seems to be abnormal

___ ___ ___ **5.** Pitch seems to be abnormal

___ ___ ___ **6.** Other_____

FLUENCY PATTERNS

L1 L2 D

___ ___ ___ **1.** Appropriate

___ ___ ___ **2.** Speech very slow and uneven

___ ___ ___ **3.** Speech more hesitant and jerky than a native speaker of the same age

___ ___ ___ **4.** Abnormal number of repetitions, prolongations, or stoppages in speech pattern

___ ___ ___ **5.** Other_____

*Whenever the terms *unusual* or *abnormal* are noted, discuss in detail the reasons for the notations. These terms suggest that the utterance is inappropriate for the language/dialect being assessed.

5

(e) AUDITORY ACUITY: Passed screening _____   Failed screening _____

(f) AUDITORY COMPREHENSION

L1 L2   D

___ ___ ___   1. Understands everything in both formal and colloquial speech expected of a native speaker of the same age.

___ ___ ___   2. Understands everything in conversation except for colloquial speech.

___ ___ ___   3. Understands somewhat simplified speech directed to him, with some repetition and rephrasing.

___ ___ ___   4. Understands only slow, very simple speech on concrete topics; requires considerably more repetition and rephrasing than would be expected of a native speaker of the same age.

___ ___ ___   5. Understands too little for the simplest type of conversations.

6

MORPHOSYNTACTIC ANALYSIS (from language sample)

Note the client's nonnative (acquired English) or nonstandard grammatical patterns; also rate the client on the accompanying grammar scale.

1. Morphologic Problems

L1 L2 D
__ __ __ **a.** noun forms
__ __ __ **b.** adjective
__ __ __ **c.** verb forms
__ __ __ **d.** adverb

2. Syntactic Problems

L1 L2 D
__ __ __ **a.** word order
__ __ __ **b.** questions
__ __ __ **c.** negation
__ __ __ **d.** prepositions
__ __ __ **e.** pronouns
__ __ __ **f.** subject–verb
__ __ __ **g.** present for future

3. Grammar Scale:

L1 L2 D
__ __ __ 1. Normal standard English grammar.
__ __ __ 2. Few errors, with no patterns of failure, but still lacking full control over grammar that is expected of that age.
__ __ __ 3. Occasional errors showing imperfect control of some grammatical patterns but no weakness that causes misunderstanding.
__ __ __ 4. Frequent errors showing lack of control of some major patterns and causing more misunderstanding than would be expected for a native speaker of that age level.
__ __ __ 5. Grammar almost entirely inaccurate except in common phrases.

FOR THE CLASSROOM TEACHER   **7**

Please Check and Discuss Any Information of Relevance

Child's Name _____ | CHILD IS:
Age_____ Sex_____ | *Nonnative English Speaker* _____
Address_____ | 1. Spanish Influenced English _____
Grade Level_____ | 2. Asian Influenced English _____
 | 3. Other _____
School _____ | *Nonstandard English Speaker* _____
Address_____ | 4. African Influenced English _____
 | 5. Appalachian Influenced English ___
 | 6. Other _____

Discuss:
Intelligibility (Understandability) of the Child

Amount of Dialect/Language Differences Used by Child in the Classroom

Estimate the amount of dialect/language differences (from minimal or none to maximum on following scales

I_I_I_I_I	I_I_I_I_I	I_I_I_I_I	I_I_I_I_I	I_I_I_I_I	I_I_I_I_I
1 2 3 4 5	1 2 3 4 5	1 2 3 4 5	1 2 3 4 5	1 2 3 4 5	1 2 3 4 5
Phonology or Articulation Usage	Grammar	Vocabulary	Prosody or Speech Rhythm	Body Language or Use of Body when Talking	Overall

USE OF LANGUAGE IN THE CLASSROOM
____ 1. Appropriate
____ 2. Opening or closing a conversation is unusual.
____ 3. Turn-taking during conversations is unusual.
____ 4. Interruptions are unusual.
____ 5. Silence as a communicative device is unusual.
____ 6. Laughter as a communicative device is unusual.
____ 7. Appropriate types of conversation are unusual.
____ 8. Humor and when to use it is unusual.
____ 9. Nonverbal behavior which accompanies conversation is unusual.
____ 10. Logical ordering of events during discourse is unusual.
____ 11. Other: _____

AUDITORY COMPREHENSION IN THE CLASSROOM
____ 1. Understands everything in both formal and colloquial speech expected of a native speaker of the same age.
____ 2. Understands everything in conversation except for colloquial speech.
____ 3. Understands somewhat simplified speech directed to him or her, with some repetition and rephrasing.
____ 4. Understands only slow, very simple speech on concrete topics; requires considerably more repetition and rephrasing than would be expected of a native speaker of the same age.
____ 5. Understands too little for the simplest type of conversations.

Appendixes

APPENDIX A

A Brief Glossary of Terms Relevant to Multicultural Communication

Aural and/or Oral Language: The segmentals, suprasegmentals (or prosody), and body movement patterns that accompany the comprehension and transmission of language symbols in differing situations.

Language Segmentals (the segments of language):

Phonology: The sounds of a language.

Lexicon: The vocabulary of a language.

Grammar:

Syntax: Sentence structure; the organization and relationship of words, phrases, or clauses in a sentence. In standard English, the adjective precedes the noun, e.g., "The President lives in the White House." In French, the adjective is positioned after the noun, "The President lives in the House White."

Morphology: The prefix and suffix; allows for the formulation of tense relationships.

Language Pragmatics: The various circumstances in which different language patterns are used; how language is used in different social situations.

Language Suprasegmentals: The pitch, stress, inflection, and intonational patterns—the speech rhythm—that accompanies the transmission of oral information (see prosody).

Body Movement: The facial and bodily movement patterns, bodily space, etc., that accompanies the transmission of oral information.

Oral Communication Patterns are primarily related to social class, ethnic membership, as well as geographical residence. Thus, middle-class speakers generally use variants of standard (network or establishment) English dependent upon the locality or region in which they have been reared. Similarly most lower-class speakers from distinctive cultures (e.g., African–American and Appalachian) use a nonstandard pattern that also may vary as a function of their geography. All of these communication systems employ a set of different linguistic and paralinguistic rules.

Bidialectal: To understand and be able to speak two different dialects. To effectively switch from one dialect to another; diglossia.

Elective Bidialectal Skills: Some protagonists of elective bidialectalism argue that (1) many students become bidialectal during the later elementary years when (2) they begin to see a need for standard English. We disagree as to the effectiveness of their standard English development when both the linguistic and paralinguistic codes are considered. We also believe that it is important for linguistic bidialectalism to develop in the early elementary years so that appropriate learning can take place in the classroom, particularly with reference to reading skills. Lastly, the amount of bidialectal proficiency achieved by these speakers is intimately related to their social class status as discussed above.

Culture: Mores, values, behaviors, including linguistic behavior, as a function of one's race, ethnicity, and social class status.

Multiculturalism in the United States:

Dominant American Culture: Euro–Americanism (white).

Nondominant American Cultures: African–Americanism (black); Asian–Americanism (yellow); Hispanic–Americanism (white, brown, black); Indian–Americanism (red) (both plains and Alaskan).

Multicultural Communicative Behaviors: The mainstream English language communicative patterns and styles of the Euro–Americans are considered to be dominant to those patterns and styles of other hyphenated Americans.

Theories Relevant to the "Inferior" Status of Members of Nondominant Cultures: Hereditarian, environmental, cultural. Language acquisition and usage by members of lower social classes are said by some to be inferior due to (1) inheritance—the genetic theories of people such as A. Jensen, W. Shockley, and others; (2) environment—the paucity of appropriate types and amounts of language stimulation and/or motivation as compared to middle-class children; (3) cultural—the members of various speech communities are provided different stimulation due to unique cultural demands. Sociolinguistic investigations show the language patterns are linguistically different and not deficient or inferior.

Dialect: The speech–language pattern used by a particular language community.

Acrolect: The most prestigious dialect.

Ideolect: An individual's dialect.

Ethnic Dialect: Varies as a function of ethnic membership and social status, such as Irish–American brogue.

Racial Dialect: Varies as a function of one's racial membership and social status, such as the African–American English of primarily the lower-class black speaker.

Regional Dialect: Varies as a function of geographical residence.

Social Class Dialect: Varies as a function of one's social class membership.

Dialect Quantity: The amount of one's social class dialect is related to the speaker's discrete sociocultural membership and the opportunity for experiencing other dialect patterns. Thus, the lower-lower-class (or underclass) member who lives within a homogenous linguistic community during his early years will generally use more nonstandard dialect than will upper-lower-class speakers who, in turn, generally will manifest more African–American English or Appalachian English than will lower-middle-class speakers.

Ethnography: The study of the behaviors manifested by a particular cultural community. The ethnography of language: the study of the language behaviors of a particular cultural group.

Linguistics: Study of language; the structure and development of a particular language.

"Prefixed" Linguistics:

Ethno: The study of the language and dialects of a given cultural group. The effect of language upon a culture and of a culture upon language.

Psycho: The study of the psychological factors involved in the perception of a response; how people use their language; the study of syntactic and semantic rules.

*Socio***:** The social class bases of language; the study of the lower-social-class dialect; the study of pragmatics or how certain peoples use language in context.

Pidgin–Creole: The former refers to the creation of a linguistic pattern between speakers of different languages that allows for communication; the latter pertains to the institutionalization of the pidgin.

Prosody: The suprasegmentals of oral language. A good example is the change in one's voice when asking a question as opposed to stating a fact. (The cat is pregnant again. The cat is pregnant again?) Not all cultures, however, use a rising inflection to convey a question or a falling inflection to convey a fact; thus, prosodic patterns are culturally bound.

Semantics: A branch of linguistics concerned with the denotative aspects of a given language.

General Semantics: A branch of linguistics concerned with the connotative aspects of a given language. Some words that have a negative connotation in standard English may not be negative when used by speakers of other dialects. How words affect behavior.

APPENDIX B

An In-Service Workshop for Teachers: Working with Multicultural Children in the Classroom

Introduction: The Need to Communicate in the Standard Vernacular of Society

I. Demographic Changes Relevant to the Multicultural (MC) Population
   A. Increasing population of MC
      1. Nonstandard speakers
         a. African–Americans
         b. Appalachian
      2. Nonnative speakers
         a. Hispanic–Americans
         b. Asian Americans
         c. Indian Americans
      3. Introduce concepts of standard vs. nonstandard (different) vs. substandard (deficient)
   B. Concerns with MC population
      1. Significant interrelationship between talking, reading, and writing
      2. Negative attitudes affecting academics and employability
      3. Strategies in the past have been ineffective in teaching children standard English
   C. Dual role of speech–language specialist and teachers in facilitating development of effective communication skills

II. Educational and Employability Problems of MC Children
   A. Lack of academic success
      1. High rate of illiteracy and concomitant high drop-out rate
      2. Research supporting damaging interrelationship between talking, reading, and writing
   B. Employability Problems

C. Possible reasons for low academic success and vocational problems
1. Environmental
2. Genetic
3. Dialect conflict
4. Negative attitudes

III. Attitudes
A. The influence of attitudes
1. Rosenthal effect
2. Hawthorne effect
B. Existing attitudes

IV. Assessment Concerns: Different vs. Deficient Speech–Language Patterns
A. Background and characteristics of dialects
1. African–American
2. Appalachian
3. Hispanic
4. Etc.
B. ASHA's position paper
C. Distinguishing between nonstandard and substandard English

V. Explanation of Three Approaches to Dialect Reduction of Nonstandard Speakers
A. Eradication
1. Pros
2. Cons
B. Nonintervention
1. Pros
2. Cons
C. Bidialectalism/Code Switching
1. Pros
2. Cons
3. Time involvement in the classroom

VI. Some Lesson Plans for the Nonstandard Speaker

VII. Accent Reduction of Nonnative Speakers

VIII. Conclusion

APPENDIX C

Assembly Bill No. 637: Passed by the California Legislature and Subsequently Vetoed by the Governor

An act to add Chapter 7.5 (commencing with Section 52190) to Part 28 of the Education Code, relating to education.

Legislative Counsel's Digest

AB 637, Hughes. Education: standard English instruction.

Existing law establishes various instructional programs in the public schools.

This bill would make standard English instruction part of the school level planning, implementation, and program review processes established pursuant to statutes and regulations governing the school improvement program, economic impact aid, and federal financial assistance to meet special educational needs of disadvantaged children. As a condition of receiving funds provided or administered by the state pursuant to those programs, each school participating in those school level planning, implementation, and program review processes that serves a student population in which 10% or more of the total pupil population lacks linguistic proficiency in standard English, including nonproficient pupils who speak a variation of English other than standard English, would be required to determine if any pupils enrolled in the school speak nonstandard English as their primary language. If that determination is positive, the bill would require the school to include specified plans regarding standard English instruction in the school planning process.

This bill would create an advisory committee on standard English comprised of specified representatives, to assist the superintendent in the development and implementation of model criteria for standard English instruction and activities.

The bill would require the Superintendent of Public Instruction to develop, and the State Board of Education to adopt, rules and regulations necessary to implement the bill, regarding specified matters, on or before April 1, 1986.

This bill would state the Legislature's intent that activities related to standard English instruction established pursuant to the provisions of this bill be funded through existing funding to public schools.

The people of the State of California do enact as follows:

SECTION 1. Chapter 7.5 (commencing with Section 52190) is added to Part 28 of the Education Code, to read:

CHAPTER 7.5. STANDARD ENGLISH INSTRUCTION

52190. The Legislature finds and declares all of the following:

(a) Many varieties of English are linguistically different from standard English and may impede many students' educational achievement.
(b) The failure of many children in various subject areas and their low performance on proficiency examinations and standardized tests can often be traced to their limited proficiency in standard English.
(c) Practicing standard English as a systematic part of the instructional program can maximize a student's ability to speak, read, and spell standard English.

52191.

(a) Standard English instruction shall be part of the school level planning, implementation, and program review processes established pursuant to the statutes and regulations governing the school improvement program, economic impact aid, and federal financial assistance to meet special educational needs of disadvantaged children (Sec. 3801 et seq., subch. 1 (commencing with Sec. 3801), Ch. 51, Title 20, U.S.C.).

(b) Each school participating in the school level planning, implementation, and program review processes specified in subdivision (a) that serves a student population in which 10 percent or more of the total pupil population lacks linguistic proficiency in standard English, including nonproficient pupils who speak a variation of English other than standard English, shall, on a cyclical basis during the school planning process, as a condition of receiving funds provided or administered by the state pursuant to the programs specified in subdivision (a), do all of the following: (1) Determine if any pupils enrolled in the school speak nonstandard English as their primary language. (2) If the determination made pursuant to paragraph (1) is positive, the school planning process shall include, but not be limited to, plans to ensure that the school activities include all of the following:

(A) Oral language instruction, including structured and spontaneous oral language practices in standard English on an ongoing basis and an oral language component in all curricula.

(B) Special instructional strategies to teach standard English to pupils, such as: (i) Storytelling, oral book reports, oral word games, oral reading, oral mathematics, and listening activities to provide participants with basic skills for successful performance in other academic disciplines requiring oral and written proficiency in standard English. (ii) Drill and practice in the phonological and grammatical aspects of standard English which differentiate it from other types of English.

(C) Staff development activities relating to standard English instruction.

(D) Activities and information for parents regarding the implications of educational strategies to address the linguistic needs of program participants.

52192.5. An advisory committee on standard English is hereby created to assist the Superintendent of Public Instruction and the State Board of Education in the development and implementation of model criteria for standard English instruction and activities. The committee shall be appointed as follows:

(a) One representative appointed by the President of the University of California.

(b) One representative appointed by the Chancellor of the California State University.

(c) From the following groups, three representatives appointed by the Superintendent of Public Instruction, two representatives appointed by the Speaker of the Assembly, and two representatives appointed by the Senate Rules Committee:

(1) Public postsecondary educational institutions.
(2) Elementary school administrators.
(3) Secondary school administrators.
(4) Elementary school teachers.
(5) Secondary school teachers.
(6) Parents of elementary school pupils.
(7) Parents of secondary school pupils.

Except for parent members, each member of the advisory committee shall be experienced in, and knowledgeable about, linguistics. The advisory committee shall serve without compensation.

52193. On or before April 1, 1986, the Superintendent of Public Instruction shall develop, and the State Board of Education shall adopt, rules and regulations necessary to implement this chapter, regarding all of the following:

(a) Necessary revision of the school level planning, implementation, and review process to implement this chapter.

(b) The provision of technical assistance to school districts and county offices of education in the planning, implementation, and review of standard English instruction.

(c) Procedures to identify effective components of standard English instruction, and disseminate information regarding those components to every school district and county office of education in the state.

52194.   It is the intent of the Legislature that activities related to standard English instruction established pursuant to this chapter be funded through existing funding to public schools, in order to impose no additional costs upon the state.

The Governor's Veto Message

I am returning Assembly Bill No. 637 without my signature.

AB 537 would require that standard English instruction be part of the school level planning, implementation, and program review processes currently established for the School Improvement Program (SIP), Economic Impact Aid (EIA) and federally funded ECIA Chapter I (Compensatory Education) programs as a condition of receiving funds provided by or administered by the State. Further, the bill would require that those schools identifying more than 10 percent of their pupils as lacking linguistic proficiency in English, as a condition of receiving EIA, SIP and Federal ECIA Chapter I funds, establish a Standard English Instruction program as outlined in the bill.

The 1985–86 Budget Act provides over $895 million for compensatory education programs for children experiencing learning difficulties in specific subjects including English. This bill would redirect the use of State and federal funds which are now available to local education agencies for their discretionary use, by imposing a costly language assessment on school districts. Consequently, funds would be shifted from program areas to pupil assessments.

In addition, AB 637 does not define "standard English" nor specify how schools will conduct a "standard English" assessment. Furthermore, I do not believe the State has the authority to mandate the use of Federal Compensatory Education funds for the bill's activity.

APPENDIX D

Policy Document of the California State Board of Public Instruction and the Los Angeles Proficiency Program for the Black Learner

Policy Document of the California State Board of Public Instruction*

Many Black learners come to the school setting speaking a language that is linguistically different from standard English. The language they speak is an integral part of the Afro–American culture . . . . It is a uniquely rich language which serves a uniquely rich culture. However, the school setting and that of the larger American society, including the economic and commercial communities, represent another linguistic sphere in which the student must learn to move and speak successfully. To the extent that the young student fluently communicates in either language, he increases his opportunities in both realms . . . .

Therefore, to provide proficiency in English to California students who are speakers of Black language and to provide equal educational opportunities for these students, it is recommended that: the State Board of Education and the State Department of Education hereby recognize:

That structured oral language practice in standard English should be provided on an ongoing basis.

That special program strategies are required to address the needs of speakers of Black language.

That parents and the general public should be informed of implications of educational strategies to address the linguistic needs of Black students.

---

*The text of this document is presented in more detail as Appendix F on page 157.

That this effort to improve proficiency in standard English for speakers of Black language *is not*: (1) a program for students to be taught to speak Black language; (2) a program for teachers to learn to speak Black language; (3) a program requiring materials in textbooks to be written in Black language . . . .

Therefore, the State Board of Education and the State Department of Education, with the adoption of this policy statement, provide direction and leadership to the districts and schools of the State of California in the development and refinement of proficiency in English programs for speakers of Black language.

Proficiency in English Program (P.E.P.) for the Black Learner†

Overview

The *Proficiency in English Program (P.E.P.)* is designed to provide supplemental assistance to Chapter 1 schools in the implementation of their ongoing oral language development programs to increase oral language competence and effectiveness. The P.E.P. curriculum aims at helping students to have more to say and more language with which to say it. The program will help teachers of ethnic minority students to better assist their charges in learning and using standard English proficiently.

The Proficiency in English Program has been and is one of the most successful innovative oral language development programs in existence for linguistically different students. The concept of the Proficiency in English Program has received accolades throughout the State of California and serves as the state model to various school districts seeking to implement oral language development programs for speakers of Black language. (See attached Appendix F: State Board of Education Policy Statement on Proficiency in Standard English for Speakers of Black Language, *School Program Development Manual* for Schools Funded Through the Consolidated Application, 1982.)

Goal

To raise the academic achievement level of participating students by expanding their oral language experiences using the P.E.P. model.

Objectives

- To teach standard English usage to speakers of Black language
- To have *students* develop an awareness of the importance of oral and written communication in our modern, complex society
- To enrich the students' awareness and appreciation of language differences

---

†Los Angeles Unified School District, Education Consolidation and Improvement Act/Chapter 1.

- To create students' awareness of situational appropriateness of language
- To help students become effective communicators in both their oral and written language
- To provide an awareness to *staffs* of the linguistic needs of Black students
- To provide an awareness to *parents* of the linguistic needs of Black students
- To support the district's *Basic Activities, Elementary School Curriculum* and the local school's consolidated application plan

Program Expansion Model for New Participating Schools

I. Orientation Workshop

The initial Proficiency in English Program orientation workshop to school clusters will be presented by the P.E.P. staff. This exciting workshop challenges school personnel to use innovative P.E.P. teaching strategies guaranteed to assist teachers and other staff to learn of the importance and the how-to of teaching standard English to speakers of Black language.

II. Training Process (P.E.P. trainer-of-trainers concept): The P.E.P. staff, coordinating lead training teachers (elementary/secondary), grade level training teachers (elementary), and department training teachers (secondary) will train all local school personnel on the Proficiency in English Program.

Each *elementary school* will have a coordinating lead training teacher, grade level training teachers, and two parent representatives.

Each *junior high, intermediate, and senior high school* will have a coordinating lead training teacher (from English department), department training teachers, and two parent representatives.

A. Three paid Saturday workshops (three-hour session) conducted by P.E.P. staff advisers and resource consultants for all participating coordinating lead training teachers, grade level/department training teachers, and Chapter 1 coordinators.

B. In-service training for education aides and parent representatives will be held at local school site.

III. Classroom techniques and strategies will be presented at P.E.P. demonstration schools for participating coordinating lead training teachers, grade level/department training teachers, education aides, and parent representatives by the P.E.P. staff and training teachers from the original P.E.P. demonstration schools.

IV. Schools will receive ongoing oral language lessons and resource materials.

V. Ongoing assessment and evaluation of the program will be conducted by the P.E.P. staff.

VI. Additional Enrichment Program Activities
- Parents/Community Proficiency in English Program Language Committee (two parent representatives from each school)
- P.E.P. Annual Elementary and Secondary Oratorical Contest
- Tribute—Culmination Activity

Appendix F: State Board of Education Policy Statement on Proficiency in Standard English for Speakers of Black Language

Many Black learners come to the school setting speaking a language that is linguistically different from standard English. The language they speak is an integral part of the Afro–American culture and has a combination of characteristics derived from standard English and from the origins of Black culture. It varies from region to region and reflects the many different stages and influences of the Black culture. It is a uniquely rich language which serves a uniquely rich culture. However, the school setting and that of the larger American society, including the economic and commercial communities, represent another linguistic sphere in which the student must learn to move and speak successfully. To the extent that the young student fluently communicates in either language, he increases his opportunities in both realms.

Current experiences in public schools suggest that Black students who are orally proficient in standard English tend to perform better in reading and spelling than those whose dominant speech pattern is nonstandard English.

Emphasis on the use of oral language techniques requires understanding and cooperation on the part of policy makers, administrators, instructional personnel, parents, and the students themselves. Therefore, to provide proficiency in English to California students who are speakers of Black language and to provide equal educational opportunities for these students, it is recommended that the State Board of Education and the State Department of Education hereby recognize that

- Oral language development is a key strategy which facilitates learning to achieve in reading and in other academic areas;
- Structured oral language practice in standard English should be provided on an ongoing basis;
- Oral language development should be emphasized during the teaching of reading and writing;
- Special program strategies are required to address the needs of speakers of Black language;

- Staff development should be provided for policymakers, administrators, instructional personnel, and others responsible;
- Parents and the general public should be informed of implications of educational strategies to address the linguistic needs of Black students; and
- This effort to improve proficiency in standard English for speakers of Black language **is not** *(1) a program for students to be taught to speak Black language, (2) a program for teachers to learn to speak Black language, or (3) a program requiring materials in textbooks to be written in Black language.*

Therefore, the State Board of Education and the State Department of Education, with the adoption of this policy statement, provide direction and leadership to the districts and schools of the State of California in the development and refinement of proficiency in English programs for speakers of Black language. The State Board of Education hereby declares that

- School districts should develop and implement strategies to increase proficiency in English for speakers of Black language;
- The State Department of Education, in cooperation with school districts, should provide for appropriate staff development for teachers, administrators, and other school personnel;
- Any existing general or categorical funds should be used to address these linguistic needs; and
- Local boards should adopt policies which specifically address the needs of speakers of Black language and facilitate the implementation of this state policy in their districts.

APPENDIX E

Response to a Questionnaire: Role of the Teacher Relevant to Nonstandard English Usage in the Classroom

An investigation of teachers' knowledge of multicultural issues concerning nonstandard dialects was completed in 1991. The questionnaire was given to many teachers in different school systems in eastern Tennessee counties. As can be seen by the following results, much lack of knowledge concerning these issues prevailed.

Interestingly, the only teachers who possessed some relevant information were those who had attended a workshop presented by the author. Apparently, older or younger teachers who had attended a variety of education courses in different colleges of education throughout the country possessed very limited knowledge regarding nonstandard dialectal usage, and this is in a geographical area where Appalachian (or mountain) English is commonplace.

Approximately 1,000 questionnaires were sent to school systems in many of the counties that comprise eastern Tennessee. Over 200 were returned. The teachers' perceptions of nonstandard dialect usage are indicated by their responses to the following questions.

1. From your own experience as an educator, to what degree would you characterize nonstandard dialects as

	To a Great Degree	Somewhat	A Little	Not At All
Underdeveloped primitive language	11	44	53	101
Socially useless forms that should be eradicated	10	76	42	44
Fully developed complex languages	48	38	49	113
Differing language patterns that should be maintained	18	93	59	24

2. To what degree do you believe that nonstandard dialects are the result of

Early language deprivation	53	62	48	45

	To a Great Degree	Somewhat	A Little	Not At All
Geographic/regional differences	153	59	5	2
Social class differences	110	85	15	3
Anatomical differences	7	32	51	115

3. To what degree do you believe that nonstandard dialects interfere with the speaker's ability to

Learn to read	51	99	45	22
Deal with abstract concepts	41	74	46	54
Engage in formal reasoning	29	70	49	66
Profit from instruction	34	95	44	43

4. Does your school speech–language specialist (therapist, clinician) interact with such speakers to teach them standard English-speaking skills?

29	51	43	66

5. Do you think your school speech–language specialist (therapist, clinician) should interact with such speakers to teach them standard English-speaking skills?

69	84	31	28

6. Do you think teachers should help these children learn standard English-speaking skills?

104	93	19	2

7. Are you familiar with bidialectal teaching programs?

11	35	40	131

APPENDIX F

Clinical Implications
of Cultural Differences
in Stuttering

1. It is extremely important for speech clinicians to recognize that there is no standard cultural group. Each group represents a wide variety of subcultures, depending on the degree of assimilation into the general American culture, the socioeconomic level of the subculture, the geographic location of the subculture, the educational level of the members of the subculture, and so forth. There are also individual family variations within the subculture influenced by the above-mentioned factors. Cultural orientation will only give direction to questions concerning the importance of general cultural influences. This awareness of variability will help prevent cultural stereotyping on the part of the clinician.

2. Some cultures are extremely private about their family and personal lives. The clinician should respect this privacy and not discuss such matters if the client is from such a culture.

3. Some cultures protect their children to the point where the child has great difficulty in adjusting to the school setting. This could include dealing with adults, other than family members, on a one-to-one basis.

4. Within some cultures it is impolite to speak in a "loud" voice. A child from one of these cultures might speak very softly, to the point where it is difficult to understand what is being said. This may not be shyness, but rather, a cultural influence carried over from the home.

5. Since various cultures respond to the handicapped in different ways, it is very important for the clinician to know the response of the client's culture to handicapped persons.

Source: W.R. Leith, "Treating the Stutterer with Atypical Cultural Influences," in K. St. Louis (ed.), *The Atypical Stutterer* (New York: Academic Press, 1988), pp. 30–32. Reprinted with permission.

6. Establishing rapport with the family may be difficult if the clinician is female and the culture of the family does not accept the female in this type of role. There may also be problems if the clinician is from another culture. Both of these factors may be compounded by the fact that the clinician represents a "figure of authority."

7. The role of the child within the family unit varies from culture to culture. If the cultural family unit is child-oriented, a home program may be able to be instituted, since the parents are involved with their children. However, if the cultural family unit is not child-oriented, parental cooperation is not likely to occur, regardless of attempts on the part of the clinician.

8. In cultures that are not child-oriented, the parents are usually not involved in the child's efforts in the school environment. It may be advisable to increase the rewards and encouragement the child receives in the school environment to compensate for the lack of support from the home.

9. In some cultures, the female rarely comes in contact with people of other cultures, relating only with people of her own culture. This can create problems both in terms of home visits by the clinician and the establishment of home programs.

10. There may be instances where a child is unwilling to communicate with a person of another culture. The clinician should be sensitive to this possibility.

11. Failure on the part of a child to maintain eye contact with the clinician may be a cultural factor. It should not be misinterpreted as an attitudinal sign or a secondary mannerism associated with stuttering.

12. Depending on the culture, it may not be appropriate for the clinician to touch the child. This is particularly true for some Indian tribes where the hair is considered sacred. A pat on the head would be most inappropriate with a child from such a tribe.

13. If the family is required to sign forms or other documents for the testing of a child, this may, depending on the culture, embarrass or shame the family. If this is the case, the parents may not sign the forms or documents.

14. Mannerisms used by a bilingual child to cover up his or her lack of English proficiency may be misinterpreted as secondary mannerisms associated with stuttering. The clinician should check to see if the mannerisms occur when the child is speaking his or her native language. If not, there is still a possibility that the child is stuttering while speaking English. This factor should be checked very carefully and appropriate action taken if the child is stuttering.

15. If a child is demonstrating some stuttering in his or her native language, it would be advisable to remedy the stuttering problem before enrolling the child in a program for English as a second language. Communication stress is an important factor in the development and maintenance of stuttering, and the demands for learning and speaking English would create even more communication stress on the child and make the problem worse.

*17. Communicative stress can often be found within the culture itself if oral ability is a source of peer recognition and status. Various cultures view oral ability as an important factor for status within the community. This cultural attitude can have a profound effect on the treatment of stuttering. The clinician should be aware of this factor and determine its influence on the particular child she is working with.

18. Various cultures have different attitudes towards stuttering, and it is important that the clinician determine the attitude of the family. In some cultures it is viewed as a curse or has some religious overtones. The family's attitude will have a direct influence on the treatment of the problem.

19. Many stuttering treatment programs stress the importance of eye contact as a goal of therapy. The clinician should keep in mind that this is considered a negative behavior in many cultures, particularly for the female.

---

*Number 16 was eliminated due to its nonrelevance to this text.

APPENDIX G

Pertinent Sociolinguistic Differences Among Hispanic Speakers of English as a Second Language (Grammatical and Sound Systems) and Some Spanish Demographics

Potential Negative Interference from a First Language: Spanish

The Grammatical System

Tense: Formation

Omission of *to be* in the formation of present progressive:

"He *putting* he shoes on."

Tense: Usage

Present tense response to a question in the past:

Q. What did you do to help your mother?
A. I *sweep* the floor.

Present tense response to a question in the present progressive:

Q. What's the little boy doing here?
A. He *write* in the paper.

Subject Pronoun: Usage

Omission of subject in the sentence:

Q. Why is the little boy washing his car?
A. Because is dirty.

Use of *he* in place of *she:*

Q. What's the little girl doing?
A. *He's* thinking.

Number Agreement: Subject–Verb

Use of plural verb in place of third person singular form:

"The things that he *tell* me to take him I take him."

Third person singular of "to be" used with compound subject:

"The father and the little boy *is* fishing."

Number Agreement: Antecedent

Use of plural pronoun when antecedent is singular:

Q. Why is the little boy washing his car?
A. Because *they* won't be dirty.

Possessive Pronouns: Usage

Use of definite article in place of possessive pronoun:

"They're brush *the* hair."

Use of singular possessive in place of plural possessive:

Q. What are they doing?
A. Washing *his* teeth.

Possessive: Suffix

Omission of *'s* with common nouns:

Q. Whose are they?
A. A little brother and a father.

Irregular formation with common nouns:

"The shoes *of father* and the shoes *of his brother*."

Prepositions: Substitution

Omission of *on* from *putting on:*

"He *putting* he shoes."

Omission of *at* from *look at:*

Q. What's the dog doing?
A. *Looking* the boy.

Substitutions: Miscellaneous

Use of *see* in place of *look at:*

Q. Why do you think so?
A. Because he's *seeing* the book.

Use of *washing their teeth* in place of *brushing their teeth:*

"They're *washing their teeth*."

Use of card for letter.

Spanish Words Used as Base, with English Suffixes and Pronunciation

"Seeking" for *drying* (Sp. *secar*), "*leying*" for *reading* (Sp. *leer*), "*miring*" for *looking* (Sp. *mirar*).

Position of Color Adjective and Modified Noun Reversed

"I live in that house *white*."

Misplacement of Locative Adverb

"A little girl is getting *down* the dog."

The Sound System

Substitution	Environment	Examples
1. "ch" for "sh"	all places	"chip" for "ship" "catch" for "cash" "ditch" for "dish" "latch" for "lash" "batch" for "bash"
2. "s" for "z"	all places	"rice" for "rise" "price" for "prize" "race" for "raise" "sue" for "zoo" "sink" for "zinc"
3. "t" for "th"	all places	"tin" for "thin" "tick for "thick" "pat" for "path" "mat" for "math"
4. "b" for "v"	after a nasal consonant	"embironment" for "environment" "combey" for "convey" "Dember" for "Denver" "imbite" for "invite"
5. "b" for "v"	at beginning of sentence	"ban" for "van" "boat" for "vote"
6. [β] for "b"	between vowels; at end of words	cabinet, robin, Robert, tribe, globe, lab
7. "v" for "b"	between vowels; at end of words	cabinet, robin, Robert, tribe, globe, lab

Substitution	Environment	Examples
8. "n" for [ŋ]	at end of sentence	"thin" for "thing," "sin" for "sing"
9. [ŋ] for "n"	at end of sentence	"ting" for "tin" "tang" for "tan" "bang" for "ban"
10. "n" for "m"	before "t"	"synton" for "symptom" "enty" for "empty" "sontin" for "something"
11. /i/ for /ĭ/	everywhere	"leave" for "live" "neat" for "knit" "seek" for "sick" "seep" for "sip"
12. /e/ for /æ/	everywhere	"bet" for "bat" "kettle" for "cattle" "set" for "sat" "met" for "mat"
13. /æ/ for /e/	everywhere	"pat" for "pet" "vat" for "vet" "last" for "lest"
14. /a/ for /e/	all places	all words containing /a/: "cup," "mud," "bug," "duck," "luck"
15. /u/ for /ʊ/	all places	words like put, book, look, took, shook

Spanish Demographics

States with Large Hispanic Populations

State	Percentage
New Mexico	37.8%
Texas	25.5
California	23.0
Arizona	15.3
New York	11.9
Florida	9.9
Colorado	9.7
New Jersey	8.0
Illinois	6.2

1.   Although Hispanics are expected to account for only 4% of U.S. voters, it is instructive that 90% of them live in nine of the United States and consequently have voting power in these states.

2.   Hispanics are comprised of basically three different cultural groups: Mexican–Americans, Puerto Ricans, and Cuban–Central–South Americans.

3.   Drop-out rates (from school) among Hispanics are staggering: Miami, 32%; Los Angeles, 50%; Chicago, 70%; New York, 80%. What must the schools do to attenuate these percentages? What role might the SLS play in such policy planning?

4.   A high percentage of these dropouts possess LEP English speaking skills. The SLS can play an important role regarding this problem. Significant numbers of these children have been inappropriately tested and incorrectly placed/labeled in resource or self-contained classrooms as mental retardates rather than functional or educational retardates. Why is testing inappropriate? Can you cite some laws that prohibit such unfair testing? What is our professional responsibility regarding their English-speaking skills?

5.   Our help can/should occur in consultancies to language-arts teaching programs in K–2. High school reform comes too late for most of these children. I believe we need to focus our attention and energy on the early grades and stress effective oral communications skills in English. Do you agree? If so, how can you translate this idea into effective action?

APPENDIX H

Pertinent Sociolinguistic Differences Among Asian and Hispanic Speakers of English as a Second Language

Asian–Spanish–English Vowel Sounds

The following chart compares the English vowel sounds with those of the Asian and Spanish languages. The blanks indicate nonexistent sounds.

Position	Languages	iy	iə	I	Iə	ey	eə	ɛ	ɛə	æ	æə	ə	uw	ʊ	ow	ɔ	ɔy	a	ay	aw
Initial	English	•		•		•		•		•	•				•	•	•	•	•	•
Initial	Cantonese	•				•		•		•	•				•	•	•	•		
Initial	Mandarin	•				•		•		•	•				•			•	•	
Initial	Korean							•		•		•						•		
Initial	Japanese							•										•		
Initial	Tagalog		•					•						•				•	•	•
Initial	Spanish							•										•	•	
Medial	English	•	•	•	•	•	•	•	•	•	•	•	•	•	•	•	•	•	•	•
Medial	Cantonese	•								•					•			•		
Medial	Mandarin	•								•								•		
Medial	Korean							•		•		•						•		
Medial	Japanese							•										•		
Medial	Tagalog		•			•		•						•				•	•	•
Medial	Spanish	•				•		•							•	•		•	•	
Final	English	•		•		•				•	•				•	•	•	•	•	•
Final	Cantonese	•				•		•			•				•	•	•	•	•	•
Final	Mandarin	•				•		•		•	•				•	•	•	•	•	•
Final	Korean							•	•	•								•		
Final	Japanese							•										•		
Final	Tagalog		•					•						•				•	•	•
Final	Spanish					•		•						•	•			•	•	

• denotes existence of sound

Asian–Spanish–English–Consonant Sounds

The following points should be noted from the chart: Stops in Cantonese and Mandarin are not voiced. These speakers usually perceive the voiced English stops (/b/, /d/, /g/) as voiceless unaspirated ones (i.e., /p/, /t/, /k/), and the voiceless English stops (/p/, /t/, /k/) as the voiceless aspirated ones (i.e., /pʰ/, /tʰ/, /kʰ/ as in *Peter, tea,* and *kiss*).

Position	Language	p	b	t	d	k	g	tš	dž	f	v	θ	ð	s	z	š	ž	h	l	r	m	n	ŋ	w	y
Initial	English	•	•	•	•	•	•	•	•	•	•	•	•	•	•	•	•	•	•	•	•	•	•	•	•
	Cantonese	•		•		•		•						•				•	•		•	•	•	•	•
	Mandarin	•		•		•		•						•				•	•	•	•	•	•	•	•
	Korean	•		•	•	•								•				•	•	•				•	•
	Japanese	•	•	•	•	•	•	•	•	•				•	•	•		•			•	•		•	•
	Tagalog	•	•	•	•	•	•							•				•	•		•	•	•	•	•
	Spanish	•	•	•	•	•	•							•				•	•		•	•		•	•
Medial	English	•	•	•	•	•	•	•	•	•	•	•	•	•	•	•	•	•	•	•	•	•	•	•	•
	Cantonese																								
	Mandarin																								
	Korean	•		•		•								•				•	•		•	•	•	•	•
	Japanese	•	•	•	•	•	•	•	•						•	•		•			•	•		•	•
	Tagalog	•	•	•	•	•	•							•				•	•		•	•	•	•	•
	Spanish	•	•	•	•	•	•		•					•				•	•		•	•		•	•
Final	English	•	•	•	•	•	•	•	•	•	•	•	•	•	•	•	•	•	•	•	•	•	•	•	•
	Cantonese	•		•		•															•	•	•	•	•
	Mandarin																					•	•	•	•
	Korean	•		•		•													•		•	•	•		
	Japanese																					•			
	Tagalog	•	•	•	•	•	•							•				•	•		•	•	•	•	•
	Spanish		•	•	•									•					•			•			•

• denotes existence of sound

Asian–Spanish–English Problem Sounds

The following chart summarizes those English sounds that could predictably cause problems for speakers of the respective languages because of the nonexistence or the distribution of these sounds. It may need to be pointed out again that these are not the only criteria for prediction.

Chinese	b	d	g	tš	dž	v	θ	ð	z	š	ž	r		I	æ	ʊ		
Japanese	f	x	θ	ð	l	r								I	æ	a	ʊ	ɔ
Korean	b	d	g	tš	dž	f	v	θ	ð	z	š	ž	r	I	ɛ	ʊ	ɔ	
Tagalog	tš	dž	f	v	θ	ð	z	š	ž	r				I	æ	a	uw	ɔ	ow
Spanish	dž	θ	ð	z	š	ž	h	r						I	ɛ	æ	a	ʊ	ɔ

Asian–Spanish–English Sound Substitutions

The following chart summarizes the common substitutions in the various languages.

In learning a new language it is only a natural tendency for the learner to substitute the sounds of his native language for the new sounds which he probably cannot even distinguish. Take the /θ/ sound, which does not appear in any of the languages in our study. The usual substitution is the closest sound, /s/, as in: *I think*, which becomes *I sink*; *Throw the ball*, which becomes *Slow the ball*, and *Go to the health department*, which turns out as *Go to the hells department.*

English	d	b	g	tš	dž	f	v	θ	ð	z	š	ž	h	l	r	ŋ	I	æ	ə	ʊ	ɔ
Chinese	p	t	k	tsʰ	ts		f	s	s	s/ts	s	s			l		iy	ɛ		uw	
Japenese						h	b	s	z			s		R	R		i	ε/a	a	u	o
Korean	p	t	k	tšʰ	ts	pʰ/hw	p/b	s/t	t/d	tš/dž		tš/dž		R	R		i			u	ə/o
Tagalog				ts	dy	p	b	t	d	s	s	s			r̄		i	a	a	u	o
Spanish	β	ʒ	ɣ		y/ž	β/b	s/t	s/d	s	tš	tš	x			r̄/R	n	i	a	a	u	o

APPENDIX I

The Dekalb Bidialectal Communication Program

The DeKalb Bidialectal Communication Program (DBCP) has three major objectives. The first objective is to make regular education students aware of the need for "functional flexibility" in verbal communication (i.e., the ability to use language for a variety of purposes). The second objective is to impart knowledge of the educational, social, and economic ramifications associated with the stigma of nonmainstream English communication skills. The final objective is to provide opportunities for students to develop and practice mainstream English skills that will positively impact others when impressionability is socially and academically critical. The importance and function of nonmainstream English communication skills should not be minimized. The instructional model is summarized below.

1. Preinstructional oral communication skills are videotaped for each student during reading and conversation with the teacher.

2. Student communication skills are evaluated in relation to standard English skills by the teacher. These skills are profiled by degree of organization/content of expressive language, enunciation, grammar usage, vocal tone/intonation usage, and nonverbal communication.

3. Students view videotapes of various styles of communication that have been scripted and role played through monologues and dialogues. From this activity and detailed discussions about the role plays, students develop an awareness of ineffective and effective communication skills for various situations. The concept of "home communication" (dialectal skills) and "school communication" (standard English skills) are introduced in phase three. Students then view their preinstructional oral communication videotapes with the teacher to set goals for their communication skills on their Communication Checklists. This phase is called Awareness Training.

4. Activities from the specifically developed curriculum help students practice appropriately "choosing" and "using" dialectal or standard English communication

Source: Copyright 1987 by Kelli Harris-Wright. Reprinted with permission.

skills in functional situations. The curriculum has five major teaching modules: (1) organization/content of expressive language, (2) enunciation, (3) standard English grammar usage, (4) vocal tone/intonation usage, and (5) nonverbal communication.

5. Post-instructional oral communication samples are videotaped in a "school communication" situation for each student during reading and conversation with the teacher.

6. Student communication skills are again evaluated by the teacher according to the criteria defined in number two.

7. Students view their pre- to post-communication videotapes to be made aware of their additional standard English oral communication skills.

Wright's Suggestions for Developing Standard Dialect

   I.   If it is possible, show videotapes of different verbal communicative styles, or describe and discuss:

      A. Speaking to friends

      B. Speaking to siblings

      C. Speaking to parents

      D. Speaking to teachers and other authority figures

      E. Speaking in a variety of situations, and using different communicative functions

         1. Requesting Cokes and popcorn at a football concession stand

         2. Informing the librarian that you are ready to check out your books

         3. Introducing a friend to a new acquaintance

         4. Informing a stranger at a movie that you'll be taking the next available seat

         5. Explaining to the cafeteria manager that you will have to charge your lunch today

  II. Describe the different communicative styles people use:

      A. Informal, causal, or first language code when well-known friends or family members communicate; use of some slang, idiomatic, vernacular expressions or nonstandard English features can be accepted

      B. Formal or standard dialect, when impressionability is critical and communication occurs with anyone who is not a well-known friend or family member; use of nonstandard or nonmainstream English is generally unacceptable; descriptions or elaborations of topics are often expected by the listener

         1. Talking/answering during class

2. Discussions during reading group
3. Communicating with teachers
4. Requesting/giving information to the school secretary
5. Discussions with the principal
6. Giving directions
7. Telephoning unfamiliar persons or places

III. Explain that one style of verbal communication is not superior to another style of communication. The situation in which communication will occur, and to whom, should influence the communicative style to be used.

IV. Separate speaking styles into two categories:

A. "School speech"—communication style used during school when impressionability is critical and with anyone who is not a good friend or family member; well-organized thoughts and ideas should be evident in verbal or written form

B. "Home speech"—communication style used during conversations with good friends and family members; style used among those who share similar community, social, and professional experiences

V. Define "school speech" and "home speech" at the beginning of the school year alongside the discussion of the classroom rules. Establish an expectation for which type of communicative behavior you will accept as a teacher and make your students aware of this expectation. Provide continuous feedback to your students on their use of effective or ineffective communication. Continue this process until your students' abilities to switch from "home speech" to "school speech" and the converse automatically become a part of their skills.

VI. Give students rules to follow regarding the use of standard dialect, communicative functions, and sounds in a tactful manner when rules are needed, or requested. For example,

Student's Statement: "Sherry walk home from school and never ride the bus."

Teacher's Response: 1. "Your sentence is organized; however, could you change the verbs in your sentence to "school speech?

or

2. "Your sentence could also be a "school speech" sentence. Your verbs *walk* and *ride* need an *s* at the end because they're in the present tense and your subject is singular. A "school speech" sentence would be: Sherry walks home from school and never rides the bus."

VII. Provide frequent opportunities for students to practice switching or changing their speech from "home speech" to "school speech." Opportunities to practice changing written sentences from "home speech" to "school speech" should also be given.

VIII. Allow the students to read paragraphs in "home speech" and "school speech." For "school speech," underline critical rules, standard dialectal features, or sounds that the students should focus on as they read.

IX. Provide opportunities for the students to engage in role-playing situations that include a variety of communicative styles and functions. Have the students state why they need to use one style as opposed to another style for the speaking situation. Have the students "brainstorm" words, phrases, ideas that could be most likely associated with the given situation they are going to role play to determine if their ideas are "in" or "out" of context.

X. Audio tape the students during reading and role-playing situations. Play the tape back for constructive critique. Be tactful when making comments.

XI. Videotape the students during role-playing situations whenever possible. Play the videotape back for constructive critique. Be tactful when making comments.

XII. Give all students equal opportunities to engage in various communicative activities around the school by

   A. Participating in school assembly programs
   B. Delivering morning/afternoon announcements
   C. Reading stories to the kindergarten children when free time has been earned, or as a motivator to encourage appropriate behavior
   D. Facilitating school-wide "school speech days"

APPENDIX J

The Taylor Oral Communication Program Incorporating Second Dialect Instruction

Components

1. Development of a program philosophy and set of assumptions that integrate oral communication with the total language arts program and the entire curriculum
2. Establishment of goals and grade level objectives that set priorities for instruction, and which integrate oral communication with the rest of the language arts and total curriculum
3. Development of teaching model, curriculum, and sample lessons with a three-part focus and designation of products
4. A cadre of trained personnel familiar with the culture and linguistic characteristics of the targeted population
5. Student evaluation plans and instruments
6. Staff development plan and evaluation
7. Parent/community involvement and education

Philosophy (Standard English Program)

Effective communication is a basic skill to be mastered by all students. Each student enters school with a well-developed language system that should be respected and utilized, where appropriate, by the classroom teacher in planning and implementing standard English instruction.

Students need to be taught standard English for use in those situations where its use is appropriate while, at the same time, being reinforced in the value of the home language.

Source: Orlando Taylor, Howard University, Washington, D.C. Used with permission.

Assumptions

I.   On the Role of Oral Communication in Education: Learning in the school setting is dependent upon some form of communication—spoken, written, and/or nonverbal. In general, oral communication serves as the foundation for all other types of linguistic behavior in and out of school. For these reasons,

a.   Oral communication is basic to learning in all areas of the school curriculum, as well as to the total school climate.

b.   Oral communication is associated with thinking; most ideas in the school setting are coded in verbal form. Therefore, oral communication should be integrated into the entire school curriculum.

II.   On Standard English: In a heterogeneous linguistic and cultural society such as the United States, a common ground of communication must be established for many types of information exchange. In the United States, standard English serves that purpose. Competence in this dialect provides an individual with a wider range of academic, esthetic, social, business, and professional options than would otherwise be available. One of the responsibilities of the schools is to teach all students to read, write, speak, and auditorily comprehend standard English in situations, topics, disciplines, and audiences where it is required. The acquisition of these skills is expected to provide students with a necessary tool for academic and/or career success.

III.   On Home and Community Languages: The need for a standard language as a unifying force in a heterogeneous society does not diminish, in any way, the value of the languages and dialects of the various cultural groups within a local community. These indigenous language forms not only serve as an integral cultural and historical link for all groups, they also provide an important means of expression and creativity for individual speakers. Disrespect and nonrecognition of home languages and dialects can lead to the development of negative self-concepts, poor morale, and low motivation in learners.

Respect and recognition of various types of home and community language systems need not interfere with the school's responsibility to teach standard English. In fact, respect and recognition of students' native language and dialects may even enhance the teaching of standard English dialects. Therefore, the school should:

a.   Use students' indigenous language behaviors as a basis for teaching fluency and proficiency in other language systems that are appropriate in other situations, most notably standard English.

b.   Teach students an awareness, appreciation, and respect for the beauty and value of all languages and dialects.

IV.   On the Characteristics of a Culturally Based Oral Communication Program: A culturally based oral communication program recognizes and celebrates linguistic diversity while teaching students standard English. It teaches verbal and nonverbal communication that meets the demands of different audiences, situations, and topics.

Instruction is sensitive to the aspirations and needs of the learner. It respects and builds on the culture, language, and distinct learning styles the child brings to school and responds to the need to transmit specific skills and competencies. The curriculum must be based on a sound instructional model that cuts across all phases of the curriculum and school life and utilizes, when possible, educational materials that are culturally familiar and valid. Finally, the program must contain ongoing external and self-evaluation of both the learner and the teacher.

General Principles of Second Dialect Instruction

1. Positive attitudes toward the existing language and dialect of the learner are prerequisites for a language or dialect instructional program. Positive attitudes, however, are not instructional programs in and of themselves.

2. Language or dialect instruction is best taught to learners who want to learn another language or dialect. If motivation is not present, the teacher must facilitate the acquisition of that motivation by assisting the learner to discover self-determined registers of a language or dialect.

3. Both teacher and learner must believe that it is possible to acquire another language, dialect, or socially determined register of a language or dialect.

4. Instruction in another language, dialect, or socially determined register of a language or dialect must be preceded by a nonbiased assessment of the learner's level of linguistic development within his/her own language or dialect, and his/her knowledge of the targeted language(s), dialect(s), or socially determined register(s) of a language or a dialect.

5. Selection of language and communication features to be taught in a language or communication instructional program should conform with language acquisition norms, stigmatization of features, frequency of occurrence of features, and the learner's attitudes toward the features.

6. Instruction in another language, dialect, or socially determined register of a language or dialect requires the teacher to know the linguistic and communicative rules of both the existing and the targeted language or dialect, and for the learner to be able to clearly recognize contrasts between the two.

7. Instruction in another language, dialect, or socially determined register of a language or dialect must take into account cultural factors associated with learning and teaching, including values pertaining to the roles of teachers and students, language stimuli, communicative situations, teaching materials, etc.

8. Instruction in another language, dialect, or socially determined register of a language or dialect must take into account the learning styles and preferences of the students, including preferences pertaining to group settings, learning environment, level and type of competition, affective relationships with the teacher and other learners, and level of abstractness of materials.

9. Instruction in another language, dialect, or socially determined register of a language or dialect must take into account the language goals and aspirations of the learner, his/her family, and his/her community.

10. Instruction in another language, dialect, or socially determined register of a language or dialect is best taught when explicit features of the existing language or communication system are contrasted with the targeted language, dialect, or socially determined register of a language or dialect, including rules of communicative interaction.

11. Instruction in another language, dialect, or socially determined register of a language or dialect is best taught, especially to learners whose orientations are non–Western and particularly African, when instruction in language and communication is integrated with all aspects of the living culture of the learner.

Developmental Sequence of Communication Teaching: Oral Communication Instruction Program

    I.   Positive attitude toward own language

    II.   Awareness of language varieties

    III.   Recognizing and labeling constrasting dialects

    IV.   Comprehension of meanings

    V.   Recognition of situational requirements

    VI.   Production in structured situations

    VII.   Production in controlled situations

    VIII.   Production in spontaneous situations

APPENDIX K

Mountain (Appalachian) English: A Historical Introduction and Culturally Biased Tests Favoring the Appalachian

Mountain (Appalachian) English

Hillbilly or mountain English is often considered to be the dialect of lazy and ignorant inhabitants of the Appalachian mountain region. It is, however, a rule-governed and nonstandard dialect that stems from the interactions of Scotch–Irish, and English settlers of this country.

Historically, the Scottish peoples of lower (lowland) Scotland were encouraged to outmigrate to the north of Ireland in the early 1600s. These Scotch–Irish were Protestant and their long and unabated hostilities with the southern Irish, who were Catholic, continue to this day.

Due to rising rents (from the English landowners) and poor harvests, as well as religious discrimination, they began to leave Ulster County—the northern part of Ireland—in the early 1700s, and most settled in Philadelphia. At odds with the English once again, they moved through the Cumberland Pass to Kentucky, Tennessee, North Carolina, and to the Ozarks and Missouri. An admixture of these Scotch–Irish with many German and some French migrants to these areas comprises the major inhabitants of central and southern Appalachia.

A Culturally Biased Test Favoring the Rural Appalachian*[†]

Test I

1. Ginseng or "sang" is:
   a. a leaf of a tree
   b. a square dance
   c. an herb used by the Chinese
   d. a drink made from the ginger leaf

---

*Test devised by K. Rogers and D. Stulberg as part of Operation Mainstream in Oak Ridge, Tennessee, 1970.
[†]Correct answers are given at the conclusion of Test I and Test II.

2. After it has been topped, tobacco is ready to cut when it:
   a. turns yellow
   b. is green
   c. dries
   d. turns brown

3. Women weren't allowed in a coal mine because:
   a. it was against the law
   b. it was bad luck
   c. they distracted the miners

4. When you see mice running toward the exit of a coal mine, it means:
   a. danger of a cave-in or leaking gas
   b. they're hunting someone's lunch
   c. it's going to rain

5. Red-eye gravy is:
   a. gravy with red food coloring in it
   b. gravy made with ham grease (or water and coffee)
   c. unaged moonshine
   d. fish sauce

6. Cracklin's are:
   a. made from beef
   b. pork rind and fat
   c. fireworks
   d. chicken feed

7. A twig from a small willow or sassafras limb chewed up at the end is for:
   a. chewing gum
   b. a toothpick
   c. a switch
   d. a toothbrush

8. Bee gum is:
   a. made from honey comb
   b. tree sap used for chewing
   c. an early American bee hive
   d. a sweetgum tree that attracts bees to its fruit

9. Dogwood is generally used for:
   a. a building material
   b. shuttles for looms
   c. firewood
   d. furniture

10. A barrel rim or goop and a piece of wire, "a click and a wheel," is:
    a. a child's toy
    b. a singing frame
    c. used part of a bike wheel

11. Sour mash is:
    a. a fertilizer
    b. an ingredient for moonshine
    c. a woven fence
    d. a home remedy for rheumatism

12. "Annie Over" is a:
    a. neighbor
    b. game played with a rubber ball
    c. folk tale
    d. song

13. Carbide is:
    a. added to water to make acetylene gas
    b. used to make baking powder
    c. used to make extra copies of a newspaper

14. Flax seed is used to:
    a. get something out of your eye
    b. feed chickens
    c. feed hogs

15. A pounding is:
    a. driving a nail
    b. gifts to a new neighbor
    c. a one-pound chicken

16. A peach tree fork is used for:
    a. finding oil
    b. a stirring fork in cooking
    c. finding water
    d. pruning peach trees

17. Leather britches are:
    a. threaded dried green beans
    b. britches worn by mountaineers
    c. part of a harness

18. Hogs head, ears, and sage make:
    a. sausage
    b. steamed pudding
    c. souse meat
    d. frankfurters

19. The best time for killing hogs when the meat is to be cured is:
    a. around Thanksgiving when temperature is below 32 degrees
    b. after Ground Hog Day
    c. anytime
    d. before killing frost

20. Hog jowl and black-eyed peas are:
    a. New Year's dinner eaten for good luck
    b. a remedy for the croup
    c. Thanksgiving dinner eaten for good luck

21. Sorghum is made from:
    a. sugar cane
    b. sugar beets
    c. sorghum cane

22. Lye, grease, water, and bacon rind are used for making:
    a. cracklins
    b. soap
    c. black strap molasses

23. Flying ginny is:
    a. a name of an early airplane
    b. a children's game
    c. a title of a children's story
    d. a slow mule

24. A tow sack is:
    a. a foot covering
    b. a burlap bag
    c. a foot bandage

25. Kiverlid is:
    a. a bed cover
    b. a hat
    c. a kitchen utensil

26. Flower Garden, Chicken Track, Wedding Ring, Dutch Girls are:
    a. names of songs
    b. quilt patterns
    c. square dances
    d. children's games

27. Light bread is:
    a. hot bread
    b. store bread
    c. corn bread
    d. cream puffs

28. Mole beans are:
    a. a variety of shellout beans
    b. for poisoning moles
    c. molded beans

29. An Appalachian asking for a "plug" would most likely mean:
    a. a broken down mule
    b. chewing tobacco
    c. a stopper for a sink drain

30. Johnny Johnson got his racing training:
    a. delivering groceries
    b. working as a mechanic in an auto shop
    c. delivering moonshine
    d. as a pit man at the tracks

31. "Sang," dock root, whiskey, and poke root are ingredients for:
    a. anything that ails you
    b. making moonshine
    c. country soap

32. "Long John" is the name for:
    a. underwear
    b. a famous freight line
    c. a short gun
    d. a famous literary character

33. Trees generally used for pulpwood are:
    a. dogwoods
    b. pines
    c. oaks
    d. sugar maple

34. Poke salad generally refers to
    a. berries of poke plant used for dye
    b. tender greens of poke
    c. greens bought at the store

Test II*

1. A greasy poke best serves a person who:
   a. has a cold
   b. has sore muscles
   c. is hungry
   d. is pregnant
   e. is tired

2. A dotey person is:
   a. crippled
   b. fat
   c. in love
   d. lazy
   e. senile

3. Burley is usually cured:
   a. by the processor
   b. in flue forms
   c. in open air barns
   d. on the stalk
   e. a year after it is cut

4. The word blinky refers to:
   a. a child's toy
   b. an early frost
   c. an eccentric woman
   d. soured milk
   e. spoiled canned goods

5. A bealed head refers to:
   a. a bloated cow
   b. a festering pimple
   c. a hairless condition
   d. a rotten cabbage
   e. a swollen face

6. A man who has granny trouble can look forward to:
   a. abstaining from sex
   b. the birth of his child
   c. having only daughters
   d. his mother-in-law moving in
   e. a stomach condition

7. Jumping jig refers to:
   a. dance
   b. escaped convict
   c. groom
   d. racial slur
   e. toy

8. To back an envelope is to:
   a. address it
   b. apply a return address
   c. mail it
   d. put postage on it
   e. seal it

9. A back set is a (an):
   a. brace
   b. farm tool
   c. ignorant person
   d. low chair
   e. relapse

10. Which of the following belongs least with the others?
    a. dodger
    b. grits
    c. hush puppy
    d. pone
    e. scrapple

*"Mountain Quiz," *The Mountain Call* II 1 (Christmas 1974), p. 6.

11. Southern mountain people usually express their political feelings by:
    a. voting independently
    b. seldom voting
    c. rejecting traditional candidates
    d. voting strongly Democratic
    e. voting strongly Republican

12. An anxious bench might be found in:
    a. church
    b. county jail
    c. grocery store
    d. hospital
    e. one-room school

Answers

Appalachian Test I: 1c, 2a, 3b, 4a. 5b, 6b, 7d, 8c, 9b, 10a, 11b, 12b, 13a, 14a, 15b, 16c, 17a, 18c, 19a, 20a, 21c, 22b, 23a, 24b, 25a, 26b, 27b, 28b, 29b, 30b, 31a, 32a, 33b, 34b.

Appalachian Test II: 1c, 2e, 3c, 4d, 5e, 6b, 7e, 8a, 9e, 10e, 11e, 12a.

APPENDIX L

Some Predicted Dialect Interference in Selected Language Development Tests

Northwestern Syntax Screening Test for Dialect Variation (DV)

1. The baby is sleeping.

   DV: The baby sleeping.
   The baby, he sleeping.

   The baby is not sleeping.

   DV: The baby not sleeping.
   The baby ain't sleeping.
   The baby, he not/ain't sleeping.

2. The dog is on the box.

   DV: The dog on the box.
   The dog, he up on the box.

   The dog is in the box.

   DV: The dog in the box.
   The dog, he in the box.

3. She sees the car.

   DV: She see the car.
   Her see the car.

   He sees the car.

   DV: He see the car.
   Him see the car.

Source: Presented by Walt Wolfram, Ron Williams, and Orlando Taylor at Asha Short Course, San Francisco, 1972. Reprinted with permission.

4. The cat is behind the desk.

DV: The cat behind the desk.
The cat, he/it (be)hind the desk.

The cat is under the desk.

DV: The cat (up) under the desk.
The cat, he/it (up) under the desk.

5. The boy pulls the girl.

DV: The boy pull the girl.
The boy, he pull the girl.

The girl pulls the boy.

DV: The girl pull the boy.
The girl, she pull the boy.

6. The fish is swimming.

DV: The fish swimming.

The fish are swimming.

DV: The fish swimming.
The fishes swimming.
The fish/es is swimming.

7. The girl sees the dog.

DV: The girl see the dog.
The girl, she see the dog.

The girl sees the dogs.

DV: The girl see the dogs.
The girl see the dog.
The girl, she see the dog/dogs.

8. This is their wagon.

DV: This their wagon.
This they wagon.
Here go the wagon.

This is his wagon.

DV: This his wagon.
This he wagon.
Here go the wagon.

9. The cats play.

DV: The cat play.

The cat plays.

DV: The cat play.
The cat playing.

10. Mother says, "Where is that boy?"

    DV: Mother says, "Where that boy/at?"
         Mother, she say, "Where that boy/at?"
         Mother say, "Where that boy is?"

    Mother says, "Who is that boy?"

    DV: Mother say, "Who that boy?"
         Mother say, "Who that boy is?"
         Mother, she say . . . .

11. The boy washes himself.

    DV: The boy wash hisself.
         The boy washing himself/hisself.
         The boy, he washing himself/hisself.

    The boy washes the shelf.

    DV: The boy wash the shelf.
         The boy, he wash the shelf.

12. This is my dog.

    DV: This my dog.
         This here my dog.
         Here go my dog.

    That is my dog.

    DV: That my dog.
         Tha's my dog.
         Here go my dog.

13. The car is in the garage.

    DV: The car in the garage?

    Is the car in the garage?

    DV: The car in the garage? (with question intonation)

14. The boy will throw.

    DV: The boy gonna throw.
         The boy throw.

    The boy is throwing.

    DV: The boy throwing.
         The boy, he throwing.

15. The boy jumped.

    DV: The boy jump.
         The boy, he jump.

    The boy jumps.

    DV: The boy jump.
         The boy, he jump.

16. Mother says, "Look who I found."

    DV: Mother say, "Lookit who I found."
    Mother, she say, "Look who I found."

    Mother says, "Look what I found."

    DV: Mother say, "Look/it what I found."
    Mother, she say, "Look/it what I found."

17. Has the boy found his ball?

    DV: The boy find/found the/his ball?
    Is the boy find/found the/his ball?

    The boy has found his ball.

    DV: The boy found the/his ball.
    The boy, he found his/the ball.

18. This is a baby doll.

    DV: This a baby doll.

    This is baby's doll.

    DV: This baby doll.

19. The boy is pulled by the girl.

    DV: The boy pull by the girl.

    The girl is pulled by the boy.

    DV: The girl pull by the boy.

20. The man brings the girl the boy.

    DV: The man bring the girl the boy.
    The man bring the girl to the boy.
    The man, he bring/bringing. . .

    The man brings the boy the girl.

    DV: The man bring the boy the girl.
    The man bring the boy to the girl.

Some Homophonous Word Contrasts for Nonstandard Speakers on the Wepman Auditory Discrimination Test

Form I Items		Form II Items	
dim	din	fret	threat
bum	bomb	bum	bun
clothe	clove	lave	lathe
sheaf	sheath	wreath	reef
pin	pen		

Templin–Darley Test of Articulation: Black English Responses

Word	Phonetic Symbol	Dialect Variation
pin	[I]	[I/ɛ]
bird	[ɪr]	[ɨ]
car	[r]	[ə]
pie	[aI]	[a]
boy	[ɔI]	[ɔ]
drum	[m]	[m]
spoon	[n]	[ũ]
tub	[b]	[p]
slide	[d]	[t]
dog	[g]	[k]
arrow	[r]	[ø]
bell	[l]	[U]
stove	[v]	[b]
thumb, bathtub, teeth	[θ]	[t], [f], [f]
there, feather, smooth	[ð]	[d], [v], [v]
wheel, white	[nw]	[w]
three	[θr-]	[tr]
hammer	[-mr]	[mə]
dinner	[-nr]	[nə]
paper	[-pr]	[pə]
rubber	[-br]	[bə]
doctor	[-tr]	[tə]
ladder	[-dr]	[də]
cracker	[-kr]	[kə]
tiger	[-gr]	[gə]
gopher	[-fr]	[fə]
mother	[-ðr]	[ðə]
washer	[-šr]	[šə]
arm	[-rm]	[əm]
horn	[-rn]	[ən]
sharp	[-rp]	[əp]
curb	[-rb]	[əb]
heart	[-rt]	[ət]
card	[-rd]	[əd]
fork	[-rk]	[ək]
iceberg	[-rg]	[əg]
scarf	[-rf]	[əf]
fourth	[-rθ]	[əf]
porch	[-rtš]	[ətš]
large	[-rtš]	[ədž]
apple	[pḷ]	[pU]
table	[-bḷ]	[bu]
bottle	[-tḷ]	[tU]

Word	Phonetic Symbol	Dialect Variation
buckle	[-kl̩]	[kU]
eagle	[-gl̩]	[gU]
ruffle	[-fl̩]	[fU]
whistle	[-sl̩]	[sU]
wolf	[-lf]	[Uf]
health	[-lθ]	[Uf]
nails	[-lz]	[Uz]
wasp	[-sp]	[s]
nest	[-st]	[s]
mask	[-sk]	[s]
sister	[-str]	[stə]
whisker	[-skr]	[stə]
December	[-mbr]	[mbə]
first	[-ɪrst]	[əs]
sprinkle	[-ŋkl̩]	[ŋkU]
triangle	[ŋgl̩]	[ŋgU]
twelfth	[-lfθ]	[Uf]
caged	[-džd]	[dž]
hand	[-nd]	[n]
locked	[-kt]	[k]
stopped	[-pt]	[p]
left	[-ft]	[f]
string	[str-]	[skr]
fixed	[-kst]	[ks]
jumped	[-mpt]	[mp]
month	[-ntθ]	[nt]

Goldman–Fristoe Test of Articulation

Sounds-in-Words Subtest

Item	Dialect Variation
4. gun	[gʌ̃]
7. wagon . . . wheel	[wægɔn wil]
10. scissors	[sIzə]
15. shovel	[šəbl]
16. car	[kaᵊ]
20. feather	[fɛvə]
21. pencils . . . this or that	[dIs], [dæt]
22. carrot . . . orange	[kæ ɔt]
23. bathtub . . . bath	[bæftɔːp] [bæf]
24. thumb . . . finger . . . ring	[tʌm]
34. sleeping . . . bed	[bɛːt]
35. stove	[stob]

Sounds-in-Sentences Subtest

Item	Dialect Variation
36. Je<u>rr</u>y	[jĕ°i]
ba<u>ll</u>	[bɔU]
37. ba<u>th</u>	[bæf]
38. too<u>th</u>paste	[tufpes]
42. do<u>g</u>	[dɔ:k]
43. fou<u>r</u>	[fɔ°]
fi<u>v</u>e	[fæ]
<u>th</u>irteen	[tɫ°tin]
<u>th</u>ey	[de]
44. mo<u>th</u>er	[məvə] or [mədə]

McDonald Screening Deep Test of Articulation

Item	Phonetic Symbol	Dialect Variation
2. ball, chain	bɔ[l] [tš]en	[U] [tš]
6. chair, sun	[tš]ɛ[r] [s]ən	[tš] [ə] [s]
9. star, thumb	[s][t]a[r] [θ] m	[s] [t] [ə] [t]
10. horse, key	hə[r][s] [k]i	[ə] [s] [k]
12. ear, bell	i[r] bɛ[l]	[ə] [U]
13. tree, thumb	[t][r]i [θ]əm	[t] [r] [t]
14. teeth, lock	[t]i[θ] [l]a[k]	[t] [f] [l] [k]
15. tooth, brush	[t]u[θ] b[r]ə[š]	[t] [f] [r] [š]
16. knife, spoon	nai[f] [s]pun	[s] [s]
17. leaf, chair	[l]i[f] [tš]ɛ[r]	[l] [f] [tš] [ə]
18. glove, thumb	g[l]əv [θ]əm	[l] [t]
21. mouth, tie	mav[θ] [t]aI	[f] [t]
22. watch, fork	wɔ[tš] [f]ɔ[r][k]	[tš] [f] [ə] [k]
23. fish, tooth	[f]I[š] [t]u[θ]	[f] [š] [t] [f]
28. thumb, saw	[θ]əm [s]ɔ	[t] [s]
29. saw, teeth	[s]ɔ [t]i[θ]	[s] [t] [f]
31. mouth, match	mav[θ] mæ[tš]	[f] [tš]

APPENDIX M

Assessment and Service to Normal Children with Speech–Language Differences

1. Aural Discrimination
   a. English sounds that have no counterpart in the native language
   b. English sounds that have *similar* sounds in the native language but are not the same
2. Phonology—as above
3. Morphology
   a. Morphographemic—written rules (e.g., *–ed* for past tense)
   b. Morphophonemic—spoken rules (e.g., *t* as in liked, *d* as in begged, *id* as in heated)
4. Syntax
5. Semantics
6. Prosody
7. Body Language
8. Pragmatics

Note: The communication difference may be in the native language only (L1), *or* in English (L2), *or* in both languages. Some school districts require treatment in both L1 and L2; other school districts require treatment only in L2.

For the Clinician: Some Basic Knowledge Competencies and Training/ Using a Translator

Some Basic Knowledge Competencies

1. It is desirable that you possess other language skills in addition to standard English; if not, have available appropriate interpreters (e.g., family members).
2. Have knowledge of the client's culture and heritage; if not, acquire the information. Use the library.
3. Obtain knowledge of appropriate tests to use, as well as valid testing tools and strategies.
4. Above all, develop the ability to differentiate language disorders from language differences. Thus, when a client's responses on a test are not in standard English, perform an item analysis and thereby determine, according to common usage in the client's dialect community, whether the given response is deficient or different.
5. Be sensitive to the client's use of speech prosody and body kinesics (movement). Are they different? In what ways?
6. Before implementing a particular teaching strategy (i.e., code-switching or bi-dialectalism) confer with the family and obtain their permission.

Training/Using a Translator When Interacting with Non-English-Proficient or Limited-English-Proficient Speakers

1. If possible, select an individual with competency in the regional–social basis of the language used by the client.
2. Familiarize the translator with both interview (case history) and evaluation (testing) procedures and techniques.
3. Conduct the evaluation in both the native language and English if the client is LEP.

4. Be aware of nonverbal and body language messages.
5. The translator should provide the SLS with information relevant to linguistic differences vs. deficiencies. (For example, in the client's linguistic–cultural community certain sounds may not be produced, therefore, the omission of the sound would not be deficient.) In addition, information regarding the student's culture, mores, attitudes, and behaviors should be provided to the SLS.
6. The translator may be a family member if that person possesses sufficient ability.

References

Adler, S. 1971. Dialectal differences: Professional and clinical implications. *Journal of Speech and Hearing Disorders* 36: 90–100.

Adler, S. 1973. Social class bases of language: A reexamination of socioeconomic, sociopsychological and sociolinguistic factors. *Asha* 15(1): 3–9.

Adler, S. 1979. *Poverty Children and Their Language.* New York: Grune & Stratton.

Adler, S. 1984. *Cultural Language Differences: Their Educational and Clinical-Professional Implications.* Springfield, Ill: Charles C. Thomas.

Adler, S. 1985. Comment on social dialects. *Asha* 27(4): 46.

Adler, S. 1987. Bidialectalism? Mandatory or elective? *Asha* 29(1): 41–44.

Adler, S. 1988. A new job description and a new task for the public school clinician: Relating effectively to the nonstandard dialect speaker. *Language, Speech, and Hearing Services in Schools* 19: 28–33.

Alexander v. Choate, 1985. 53 L.W. 4072. 105 sec. 712.

Alterbaum, I., and J. Buck. 1982. What about spoken English? *Asha* 24(12): 982.

Bailey, B.L. 1965. Towards new perspectives in Negro English dialectology. *American Speech* 40: 171–177.

Baratz, J. 1969. Who should do what to whom . . . and why? *Florida FL Reporter* 7(1): 158–159.

Baratz, J., and R. Shuy. 1969. *Teaching Black Children to Read.* Washington, D.C.: Center for Applied Linguistics.

Barna, Laray M. 1991. Stumbling blocks in intercultural communication. In L.A. Samovar and R.E. Porter (eds.), *Intercultural Communication,* 6th ed. Belmont, Calif.: Wadsworth Publishing Co.

Bauman, R. 1971. An ethnographic framework for the investigation of communicative behaviors. *Asha* 13(6): 334–340.

Benavides, A. 1988. High risk predictors and prereferral screening for language minority students. In A.A. Ortiz and B.A. Ramirez (eds.), *Schools and the Culturally Diverse Exceptional Student: Promising Practices and Future Directions.* Reston, Va.: Council for Exceptional Children.

Bereiter, C., and S. Engelmann. 1966. *Teaching Disadvantaged Children in the Preschool.* Englewood Cliffs, N.J.: Prentice-Hall.

Bergin, K. 1982. The relationship of English composition grades to oral (social) dialect: An analysis of dialectal and nondialectal writing errors. Master's thesis, The University of Tennessee, Knoxville, Tenn.

Bilingual Education Act, 1974. Pub. L. 98-511, 98 stat, 2369 Title 20, 3221-3223, 3231-3233, 3421-3247, 3251-3255, 3261-3262.

Bountress, N.G. 1980. Attitudes and training of public school clinicians providing services to speakers of Black English. *Language, Speech, and Hearing Services in Schools* 11: 41–49.

Brand, M. 1981. Letter to the Editor: Response to Gandour. *Journal of Speech and Hearing Disorders* 46: 218–219.

Brooks, C.K., ed. 1985. *Tapping Potential: English and Language Arts for the Black Learner.* Urbana, Ill.: Black Caucus of the National Council of Teachers of English.

Brown v. Topeka Board of Education, 1954. 347 U.S. 483.

Cole, L. 1983. Implications of the position on social dialects. *Asha* 25(9): 25–27.

Cole, L. 1985. Response to Adler. *Asha* 27(4): 47–48.

Cole, L. 1989. E pluribus pluribus: Multicultural imperatives and the 1990's and beyond. *Asha* 31(9): 65–70.

Coleman, R. and L. Rainwater. 1978. *Social Standing in America.* New York: Basic Books.

Dabney, N.L. 1983. See how it runs: A successful innercity classroom. Ph.D diss., University of Pennsylvania, Philadelphia, Pa.

Damico, J. 1985. Clinical discourse analysis. A functional approach to language assessment. In C. Simon (ed.), *Communication Skills and Classroom Success: Assessment of Language-Learning Disabled Students,* pp. 165–204. San Diego, Calif.: College-Hill Press.

Daniels, H.A. (1974). Bidialectalism: A policy analysis. *Dissertation Abstracts International* 34: 3684A-3685A. (University Microfilms No. 73-30, 569).

Diana v. State Board of Education, 1970. C-70-37 RFP, N.D. California.

Dolphin, Carol Zenna. 1991. Variables—The use of personal space in intercultural transactions. In L.A. Samovar and R.E. Porter (eds.), *Intercultural Communication,* 6th ed. Belmont, Calif.: Wadsworth Publishing Co.

Dreher, B. 1981. Letter to the editors in response to Gandour. *Asha* 24(12): 982.

Duran, R.R., M.K. Emight, and D.A. Rock. 1985. *Language Factors and Hispanic Freshmen's Student Profile,* College Board Report #85-3, ETSRR #85-44, New York.

Education of All Handicapped Children Act, 1975. Pl 94-142, 20 U.S.C. 1401.

Fasold, R.W. (1972). *Tense Marking in Black English: A Linguistic and Social Analysis.* Arlington, Va.: Center for Applied Linguistics.

Fast, J. 1970. *Body Language.* New York: Evans.

Fradd, S.H., and V.I. Correa. 1989. *Exceptional Children* 56(2): 106.

Fradd, S., A. Barona, and M. DeBaron. 1989. Implementing change and monitoring progress. In S. Fradd and M. Weismentel (eds.), *Meeting the Needs of Culturally and Linguistically Different Students.* Boston: College-Hill Press.

Frassinelli, L., K. Superior, and J. Meyers. 1983. A consultation model for speech and language intervention. *Asha* 25(11): 25–30.

Frost, J.L., and G.R. Hawkes, eds. 1970. *The Disadvantaged Child.* New York: Houghton Mifflin.

Fuchs, D., and L. Fuchs. 1989. Effects of examiner familiarity on Black, Caucasian, and Hispanic children: A meta-analysis. *Exceptional Children* 55(4): 303–308.

Galloway, C. 1970. Teaching is communication: Nonverbal language in the classroom, Document 038 069. Washington, D.C.: Educational Resources Information Center.

Gandour, J. 1980. Speech therapy and teaching English to speakers of other languages. *Journal of Speech and Hearing Disorders* 45: 133–136.

Garrard, Kay R. 1979. The changing role of speech and hearing professionals in public education. *Asha* 21(2): 91–97.

Gelfand, D.E., and D.V. Fandetti. 1986. The emergent nature of ethnicity: Dilemmas in Assessment. *Social Casework: The Journal of Contemporary Social Work* 67(9): 542–550.

Gilbert, D., and J. Kahl. 1987. *The American Class Structure: A New Synthesis.* Chicago, Ill.: The Dorsey Press.

Gillcrist, M. 1981. A rationale for providing service to the limited English proficiency student. *LSHSS* 12: 145–152.

Gleason, P. 1984. Pluralism and assimilation: A conceptual history. In J. Edwards (ed.), *Linguistic Minorities, Policies and Pluralism*, pp. 221–227. New York: Academic Press.

Glenn, M.E. 1970. *Appalachia in Transition.* St. Louis: Bethany Press.

Goelman, H. 1986. The language environments of family day care. *Advances in Early Education and Day Care* 4: 153–179.

Grimshaw, A. 1971. *Sociolinguistics: Advances in the Sociology of Language.* The Hague: Mouton.

Hall, E.T. 1976. *Beyond Culture.* Garden City, N.Y.: Doubleday.

Harber, J.R. 1979. Prospective teachers' attitudes toward Black English, Document 181 728. Washington, D.C.: Educational Resources Information Center.

Harris-Wright, K. 1987. The challenge of educational coalescence: Teaching nonmainstream English-speaking students. *Journal of Childhood Communication Disorders,* Fall-Winter, 209–215.

Hawkes, T., and R. Middleman. 1972. An experimental field study of the impact of nonverbal communication of affects on children from two socioeconomic backgrounds, Document 061 550. Washington, D.C.: Educational Resources Information Center.

Healey, W.C. 1973–1974. Standards and guidelines for comprehensive language, speech and hearing programs in the schools. Washington, D.C.: American Speech and Hearing Association.

Hechinger, Fred. 1985. "Warning over people ignoring pupils living in poverty." *The New York Times* (October 29), Sec. C, p. 11.

Heller, K., W. Holtzman, and S. Messick, eds. 1982. *Placing Children in Special Education: A Strategy for Equity.* Wasington, D.C.: National Academy Press.

Hereer, G. 1989. President's Page, The need for multicultural literacy. *Asha* 31(9): 79.

Hertzler, J.O. 1965. *A Sociology of Language.* New York: Random House.

Hess, K. 1972. Is learning standard English important? An overview. *Florida FL Reporter* 10(1-2): 39–42.

Higham, J. 1974. Another American dilemma. *The Center Magazine: A Publication of the Center for the Study of Democratic Institutions* 4: 67–70.

Hobsen v. Hansen, 1967; 1969. 269 F. Supp. 401, D.D.C.; 408 F 2nd 175, DC Cir.

Hudson, H. 1971. Foreword. In M. Imhoof (ed.), *Viewpoints,* 47(2), v–viii.

Hymes, D. 1971, 1973. Sociolinguistics and the ethnography of speaking. In E. Ardenar (ed.), *Social Anthropology and Language,* pp. 49–93. London: Tavistock.

Ima, K., and R.G. Rumbaut, 1989. Southeast Asian Refugees in American Schools: A Comparison of Fluent-English-Proficient and Limited-English-Proficient Students. *Topics in Language Disorders* (June). An Aspen Publication, Gaithersburg, Md.

Jax, V.A. 1988. Understanding school language proficiency through the assessment of story construction. In A.A. Ortiz and B.A. Ramirez (eds.), *Schools and the Culturally Diverse Exceptional Student.* Reston, Va.: Council for Exceptional Children.

Johnson, K.R. 1971. Should black children learn standard English? *Viewpoints* 47(2): 83–101.

Joiner, C. (F. Supp. 1979). *Martin Luther King Junior Elementary School v. Ann Arbor School District*, 1371–1391.

Kayser, H. 1989. Speech and language assessment of Spanish-English speaking children. *LSHSS* 20(3): 226–244.

Kleinfield, J. 1973. Using nonverbal warmth to increase learning: A cross-cultural experiment, Document 081 568. Washington, D.C.: Educational Information Resources Center.

Kochman, T. 1969. Social factors in the consideration of teaching standard English. *Florida FL Reporter* 7(1): 87–88, 157.

Kochman, T. 1971. Cross-cultural communication: Contrasting perspectives, conflicting sensibilities, Document 047 026. Washington, D.C.: Educational Resources Information Center.

Koening, L.A., and C.D. Biel. 1989. A Delivery System of Comprehensive Language Services in a School District. *LSHSS* 20(4): 338–365.

Korzybski, A. 1948. *Science and Sanity: An Introduction to Nonaristotelian Systems.* Lakeville, Conn.: International Nonaristotelian Library Publishing Company.

Labov, W. 1966. *The Social Stratification of English in New York City.* Arlington, Va.: Center for Applied Linguistics.

Labov, W. 1969. *The logic of non-standard English.* In J.E. Alah (ed.), Monograph Series on Languages and Linguistics, No. 22, pp. 1–43. Washington, D.C.: Georgetown University Roundtable on Languages and Linguistics.

Labov, W. 1972. *Sociolinguistic Patterns.* Philadelphia: University of Pennsylvania Press.

Labov, W. 1982. Objectivity and commitment in linguistic science: The case of the Black English Trial in Ann Arbor. In D. Hymes, (ed.), *Language in Society,* pp. 165–201. Cambridge: Cambridge University Press.

Lampe, P.E. 1988. The problematic nature of interracial and interethnic communication. *The Social Studies,* May/June.

Larry P. v. Riles, 1979; 1984. 495 F. Suppl. 926, N.D. California; 83-84 EHLR DEC. 555:304, California.

Lau v. Nichols. 1974. 94 Supreme Court, 786, Calif. 414, US563.

Leith, W.R. 1988. Treating the stutterer with atypical cultural influences. In K. St. Louis (ed.), *The Atypical Stutterer,* pp. 9–33. New York: Academic Press.

Loban, W. 1966. Problems in oral English. *NCTE Research Reports* 5.

Lora v. State Board of Education, 1984. Final ruling: 587 F. Suppl. 1572, E.D.N.Y.

MacKay, I.R. 1978. *Introducing Practical Phonetics.* Boston, Mass.: Little, Brown.

Marckwardt, A.H. 1971. Concept of standard English. In *Discovery of English,* pp. 13–16. Urbana, Ill.: NCTE Distinguished Lectures.

Marshall v. McDaniel, 1984. Civil No. 482-233, D.D., Georgia.

Martin Luther King Junior Elementary School Children v. Ann Arbor School Distict Board, 1979. 473 F. Supp. 1371.

Mattes, L., and D. Omark. 1984. *Speech and Language Assessment for the Bilingual Handicapped.* Boston: College-Hill Press.

Mattie T. v. Holladay, 1979. 3 EHLR 551:109, N.D., Mississippi.

May, Lee. 1979. "Black English." *Atlanta Journal and Constitution,* Sunday Magazine (June 24), pp. 22–27.

McCrum, R., W. Cran, and R. MacNeil. 1986. *The Story of English.* New York: Viking Press.

McCartney, K. 1984. Effect of quality of day care environment on children's language development. *Developmental Psychology* 20(2): 244–260.

McNett, I. 1983. *Demographic Imperatives for Educational Policy.* Washington, D.C.: American Council on Education.

Mehrabian, A. 1969. Communication without words. In *Readings in Psychology Today.* Del Mar, Calif.: CMR Books.

Mellan, O. 1970. Why try to eradicate it? *The New Republic* 163(22): 15–17.

Mercer, J. 1976. Pluralistic diagnosis in the evaluation of Black and Chicano children: A procedure for taking sociocultural variables into account. In C. Hernandez, M. Haug, and N. Wagner (eds.), *Chicanos: Social and Psychological Perspectives,* pp. 193–195. St. Louis, Mo.: C.V. Mosby.

Olson, L. 1988. The unbalanced equation. *Education Week,* June 22, pp. 19–20, 22–23, 26.

Ortiz, A., and E. Polyzoi. 1988. Language assessment of Hispanic learning disabled and speech and language handicapped students: Research in progress. In A.A. Ortiz and B.A. Ramirez (eds.), *Schools and the Culturally Diverse Exceptional Student: Promising Practices and Future Directions.* Reston, Va.: Council for Exceptional Children.

Ortiz, A., and J. Yates. 1983. Incidence of exceptionality among Hispanics: Implications for manpower planning. *Journal of the National Association for Bilingual Education,* 41–53.

PASE v. Hannon, 1980. 506 F. Suppl. 831, N.D. Illinois.

Pavenstedt, E. 1965. A comparison of the child-rearing environment of upper-lower and very lower-class families. *American Journal of Orthopsychiatry* 35: 89–98.

Peins, M., N. Colburn, and N. Goetz. 1984. The SESL model. *Asha* 26(11): 47–50.

Quinn, J. 1985. Linguistic segregation. *The Nation* 241: 479–482.

Ramirez, B.A. 1988. Culturally and linguistically diverse children. *Teaching Exceptional Children* 20: 45–51.

Robey, B. 1984. Emerging black ethnics. *American Demographics* 11.

Rowan, C. 1979. Black English nonsense. *The Oak Ridger,* July 12, p. 5.

Rehabilitation Act, 1973. 29 U.S.C. 794.

Rueda, R., D. Cardoza, J. Mercer, and L. Carpenter. 1985. Fund Report: Contract #300-83-0273, Washington, D.C., U.S. Department of Education. As cited in Jax, V. 1988. Understanding school language proficiency through the assessment of story construction. In A.A. Ortiz and B.A. Ramirez (eds.), *Schools and the Culturally Diverse Exceptional Student.* Reston, Va.: Council for Exceptional Children.

Scott, J.C. 1985. The King Case: Implications for Educators. In C.K. Brooks (ed.), *Tapping Potential: English and Language Arts for the Black Learner,* pp. 63–71. Urbana, Ill.: Black Caucus of the Natitonal Council of Teachers of English.

Shuy, W.R. 1972. Social dialect and employability: Some pitfalls of good intentions. In L.M. Davis (ed.), *Studies in Linguistics,* pp. 145–156. University of Alabama: University of Alabama Press.

Sledd, J. 1969. Bidialectalism: The linguistics of white supremacy. *English Journal* 58: 1307–1315.

Smitherman, G. 1985. What go round come round: Keep in perspective. In C.K. Brooks (ed.), *Tapping Potential: English and Language Arts for the Black Learner,* pp. 41–62. Urbana, Ill.: Black Caucus of the National Council of Teachers of English.

Tarone, E. 1972. Aspects in Intonation in Black English, Document 076983. Washington, D.C.: Educational Resources Information Center.

Terrell, S., and F. Terrell. 1983. Effects of speaking Black English upon employment opportunities. *Asha* 26: 27–29.

Vaughn-Cooke, F.B. 1983. Improving language assessment in minority children. *Asha* 25(9): 29–34.

Watson, L. 1989. A comparison of the types of utterances used by mothers and day care workers to infants. Master's thesis, The University of Tennessee, Knoxville, Tenn.

Weiner, F.D., G. Bergen, and D.K. Bernstein. 1983. Nonnative English speakers. *Asha* 25: 18–22.

Williams, R. 1976. The anguish of definition: Toward a new concept of blackness. In T. Trabasso and D.S. Harrison (eds.), *Black English: A Seminar*. Hillsdale, N.J.: LEA Publishers.

Wolfram, W., and D. Christian, 1975. *Sociolinguistic Variables in Appalachian Dialects*. Arlington, Va.: Center for Applied Linguistics.

Wolfram, W., and R.W. Fasold. 1974. *The Study of Social Dialects in American English*. Englewood Cliffs, N.J.: Prentice-Hall.

Wolfram, W., L. Potter, Yanofsky, and R. Shuy. 1979. *Reading and Dialect Differences*. Arlington, Va.: Center for Applied Linguistics.

Yates, J. 1988. Demography as it affects special education. In A.A. Ortiz and B.A. Ramirez (eds.), *Schools and the Culturally Diverse Exceptional Student: Promising Practices and Future Directions*. Reston, Va.: Council for Exceptional Children.

Yoder, D. 1970. Some viewpoints of the speech, hearing and language clinician. In F. Williams (ed.), *Language and Poverty*. Chicago, Ill.: Markham Publishing Company.

Young, V.H. 1970. Family and childhood in a southern Negro community. *American Anthropology* 72: 269–288.

Index

Ability, and dropouts, 16
Acculturation. *See* Assimilation; Cultural assimilation
Achievement
  and communication, 125
  and dialect speaker, 24
  and language proficiency, 126
Achievement, low
  and dialectal difference, 15
  and educational programming, 77
  and LEP speaker, 124
Acrolect, 145
Adjectives, in African–American English, 59
Adler, S., 7, 9, 12, 19, 24, 26, 40
Adverb, in African–American English, 59
African–American
  and labeling, 36
  population, 1
  and social mobility, 102
  and test bias, 86
African–American English, 49
  debate, 20
  and dialect, 49, 52
  and employment, 20, 28n.6
  and language proficiency, 157–158
  linguistic system of, 55–59
  and need for standard English, 20
  negative perception of, 19, 21, 25
  origin of, 50
  and P.E.P., 155–156
  and racism, 28n.6
  specifics of, 53, 55–59, 71–75
  and stereotype, 28n.6
  teachers' acceptance of, 101
  and Templin-Darley Test of Articulation, 190–191
African–American speaker, and code switching, 12
Alexander v. Choate, 78
Alterbaum, I., 123
American Speech–Language–Hearing Association

and eradication strategy, 9–11
Americanization. *See* Assimilation
"Anguish of Definition: Toward a New Concept of Blackness, The" (Williams), 49n
Ann Arbor Case, 19, 20–21, 26, 81
Appalachia, inhabitants of, 181
Appalachian
  and social mobility, 102
  and test, culturally biased, 181–185
Appalachian English, 49, 53
  and attitudinal barrier, 21, 26–27
  and dialect, 52
  history of, 181
  linguistic system of, 59–62
  negative perception of, 25
  specifics of, 53, 59–62, 71–75, 100–101, 107–108, 110–122
  teachers' acceptance of, 101
Appalachian school system, and bidialectal teaching strategy, 27
Araucanion, 49
Articulation, and TESL, 133
Asha, 6, 11
ASHA. *See* American Speech-Language-Hearing Association
Asian–American
  population, 134
  and sociolinguistic difference, 169–172
Asian/Pacific Islander–American, 1
Assembly Bill No. 637, 150–153
Assessment, language. *See* Language assessment
Assessment Instrument
  communicative aspect of, 134
  and language proficiency, 124–125
  for multicultural client, 133
  specifics of, 136–142
Assimilation, 21–22, 161
Attitudinal barrier
  and Appalachian English, 21, 26–27
  and bidialectal–bicultural program, 86
  and dialect speaker, 15